PEACE SPIRITUALITY
FOR
PEACE MAKERS

Dom Helder Camara . Mgr. Luigi Bettazzi . Mgr. Paul Schruers .
Bernard Cardinal Alfrink . Prof. Dr. Edward Schillebeeckx o.p. .
Prof. Dr. Richard Friedly o.p. . Prof. Dr. Enrico Chiavacci .
Mary Evelyn Jegen s.n.d. . Prof. Joseph Comblin .
Jean-Marie Müller . Prof. Gerard A. Vanderhaar .
Dom Benoit Standaert o.s.b. . Dom C.J.A. Tholens o.s.b. .
Dom Thomas Cullinan o.s.b. . Fr. Donal O'Mahony o.f.m.cap.

Made and printed in Belgium
Ed. OMEGA, Kerkstraat 150, B-2008 Antwerpen.

D/1983/3948/4
ISBN 90 70316 23 4

PREFACE

Injustice and the increasing arms race threaten the future of our world.

Will we react in time? Dom Helder Camara put this question many years ago.

Today we experience in a very special way the challenge to commit ourselves more than ever to world peace and justice. But as Christians we realise that our commitment to justice and peace has to be based on prayer and the World Incarnate. Peace is our historical mission, but for believers, God, as Source of all peace, has to permeate all our activity.

The International Catholic Peace Movement realises the need of linking contemplation with action for peace. This Pax Christi book provides stimulating starting points for discussion leading to a thorough theological and spiritual study of peace work in its widest sense, therefore contributors to this book include bishops, theologians and committed Christians.

This book is a result of the Pax Christi International Congress on Peace Spirituality which took place in Nassogne (Belgium) from 9-11 October, 1981. The presence of 250 participants from 20 countries at this Congress made possible a very rich exchange of experiences. Thanks to the hard work of many people and especially of Pax Christi Wallonia-Brussels, the Congress was a success.

It was a strong stimulus to the international movement of Pax Christi to be able to look for new forms of Peace Spirituality and to continue its study of the link with the 'Gospel of Peace' (Eph. 6:15).

By publishing this book Pax Christi hopes to contribute to a contemporary Peace Spirituality, the essence of which is our mission to become, with the whole Church real peacemakers, inspired by the peace of Christ.

Jo Hanssens, in the name of the ad hoc working-group 'Peace Spirituality' of Pax Christi International.

4

Contents

Dom Helder Camara
A MULTINATIONAL OF FAITH, HOPE AND LOVE

1. Excuse me if I am wrong...

I am quite happy, dear brothers and sisters, to be with you to meditate for a few moments on the theme of this Congress of Pax Christi International. I feel quite at ease for I am convinced that you are talking about an incarnate spirituality. We are no angels, no pure spirits. We are human creatures: spirit and body. I never feel a shepherd of souls only: the Lord has made me a shepherd of human creatures: soul and body. Of course, it is also true the other way round: I never feel a shepherd of bodies only. May the Spirit of God help us in the difficult task of talking to bodies, which are the flesh that we received from our parents, in a splendid moment of love; but a flesh imbued with a spirit intentionally created to measure by God, in order to be one with our body.

2. Synthesis of a divine audacity

Only the Creator and Father could go as far as uniting spirit and body. Only God could make body and spirit one within ourselves. We are simultaneously mortal and immortal. At the same time we are limited and finite, but we long for the infinite, the absolute, the eternal. It is impossible to forget that we are dust on our tiny Earth, dust in the cavalcade of stars. But it is also impossible to forget that God has made us partake in His divine intelligence and His creating power. He has made us co-creators, entrusted with mastering nature and completing the creation.

The tragedy is that on the level of intelligence, we have always proved and we still prove, even more than ever before, that we really partake in the divine nature and that we are co-creators... But on the level of egoism, it is true that we remain animals, beasts, and wild beasts...!

3. A decisive test

War and peace: this is a decisive test in order to establish whether within ourselves the body chokes the spirit, whether the beast forgets the brother of the angels, and whether we have chosen to behave as little gods by trying to reduce the whole of nature to slavery and by becoming experts in destruction.

War has always been animal, bestial, and even more than that. One animal kills another in order to have something to eat, never because of hatred... Try to imagine a tiger preparing for a war of tigers against lions or, even worse, of tigers against other tigers.

Why should we conclude that, when killing, devastating and tearing even more, we prove that we were right and that God, therefore, has helped us?!

4. War, which has always been stupid, becomes absurd

Only God is the Lord of life and he has told us not to kill.

Killing someone in everyday life is a crime. Killing during a war is an act of heroism, that deserves congratulations and even decorations, according to the number and rank of the people who have been killed. In the evolution of war, mortality has been increasing. Nowadays, because of bombing, towns and their populations very often suffer even more than the soldiers.

But it is really the atomic bomb — I mean nuclear weapons — that makes war stupid. Or, to be more precise, the stupid character that wars have always had becomes even clearer and more undeniable.

What we spend on nuclear armaments is insane: one million US dollar every minute, 450 thousand million US dollar every year.

Even more insane is the ever-increasing destructive power of those weapons:
- *a nuclear submarine equipped with 20 missiles, such as the new Trident, can completely destroy 408 towns like Hiroshima and Nagasaki...*
- *both sides, the United States of America and the Soviet Union, possess over sixty times what is necessary to destroy life on our planet...*
- *twice in 1980, a mistake made by a North-American computer nearly set off a nuclear war between the capitalist and communist superpowers, with unpredictable consequences...*

5. *It seems, apparently, useless to make war against war*

Thinking of abolishing war seems useless, impossible and naive. The multinationals cannot admit even the mere thought of the abolition of wars. How could one give up such a tremendous industry, even though it is designed to produce death? The multinationals manipulate the means of social communication: newspapers, magazines, books, radio and television stations, advertising agencies... in order to prove that national security is the supreme value for each nation. For research in the field of the armaments (nuclear weapons in particular) expenditure is perfectly acceptable. It is even necessary.

Schools designed to prepare wars have an increasing ability to indoctrinate youth by drawing them into the spiral of violence, into the madness of always wanting to beat records of destruction, into the heresy of regarding themselves as the Lord of life and death.

6. *A huge force with incomparable energies*

The year 2000 of the Incarnation of Christ is very close now. What a big challenge for us, Christians, who know about the miserable balance-sheet of the first 2000 years of Christianity, as a consequence of our Christian weakness:

- *the countries (a very small minority) that become increasingly rich because they dominate more than two thirds of mankind, are at least in origin Christian countries;*
- *the Christian part of the poor world — Latin America — shows the same situation of injustice as there is in Europe and North America, two Christian areas;*
- *on the eve of the year 2000, more than two thirds of mankind suffer from misery and hunger. Last year, 50 million people died of starvation;*
- *we can clearly see the terrible injustice caused by international trade policies; the consumer society wastes the raw materials of the Third World; the multinationals exert an imperialist domination.*

We must encourage our various Christian denominations to try and see what brings us together, rather than what separates us. We can immediately ask all those who are believers and regard God as the Father of all human creatures, of all races, of all colours, of all religions and even of the unbelievers who love the human creature and who already love, unknowingly and maybe without wanting to do so, the Creator and Father, to join us.

7. Coming into operation, the multinational of Faith, Hope and Love

Let us remind ourselves of the major truths of our peace spirituality:
- *God is love. The best way to honour God is to keep love alive inside and around ourselves.*
- *We must beware of the egoism that we all bear inside ourselves. Sometimes it is dozing. It might even give the impression that it has died... That is only an illusion.. It is the egoism that results from the insatiable greed of having, having, having ... There is individual, family, professional, regional, national, multinational egoism ...*

- *In areas of poverty, of oppression, and even in inhuman areas, the Spirit of the Lord inspires us to work, not only for the people, but with the people. As long as we only work for the people, we are still the strong, the able, the powerful who are so generous as to help the people. Now, if we work with the people, we recognize their value and we discover, even among the illiterate, the ability to think, to judge and to act in an intelligent and accurate way.*
- *In industrial and rich countries, the Spirit of God stimulates an increasing number of small groups, especially among the youth:*
  - *who take it as given that, in every country, the number of people of good will is higher than one could have imagined;*
  - *who try and help raise the consciousness of these people of good will, who very often lack good information on the real condition of mankind.*

The spirituality of peace makes us sure that, in spite of the appearance to the contrary, there are millions gathered around God, who consider God as our Father. We are:
- *the people who pray, but also the people who vote;*
- *the people who live on faith, hope and love, but also the people who pay taxes, and that is the reason why the means of social communication exist;*
- *people who reject hatred an violence, but who can exert a liberating moral pressure.*

If Pax Christi International thinks it is advisable to do so, it can recognize and proclaim — without any bureaucratic or financial obligation — the existence of the multinational of Faith, Hope and Love.

A multinational of Faith, more necessary than ever before in this hour of supreme danger when humanity is falling back into the absurdity and the madness that lies in thinking we can do without God, and in changing our role as co-creator, which was evidence of the goodness and mercy of God, into the role of a creator who does not feel the need for the presence of God.

A multinational of Hope, more necessary than ever before, in this moment when the lack of hope and even the total absence of it is threatening millions of human beings who live in a sub-human condition of misery and hunger, whereas the very small minority is so rich that they do not even know what to do with so much money and they are scared to death of the M-bomb, the bomb of Misery, that is even more terrible than the nuclear bomb and the clean, devilish bomb called neutron bomb.

A multinational of Love that is invincible because, in our world that was created by God who is Love, Love will overcome egoism, the latter being the last obstacle that is responsible for the injustice that makes true and lasting peace impossible; it will overcome hatred, on which nothing can be built; it will overcome violence, which threatens to take us into a spiral of violence.

Praise be to our Creator and Father for the creation of the Multinational of Faith, Hope and Love.

Mgr. Luigi Bettazzi
THE RESPONSIBILITY OF THE CHRISTIAN
COMMUNITY

It is with some emotion that I open this congress on peace spirituality: emotion and gratitude towards God, of course, who allows us to meet and look into what is the very reason for our movement: the religious, evangelical inspiration of our commitment to peace.

But I am also very grateful to all those who have accepted to come — from very far sometimes — and guide our reflection. Also allow me, dear bishops, theologians, women and men with a Christian experience, to thank in particular Don Helder Camara who, from his country, Brazil — and I can even add, from the whole world — has brought the call of the poor, of the outcasts, of those we forget about, who ask the rich countries, the so-called 'developed countries', to build peace by achieving justice.

At the beginning of this congress, I would like to stress that I believe he plays an important role in the life of our movement and, I would even say, in the life of the Church and of the world. The arms race between the powerful has brought together so many weapons — frightening weapons that can wipe out any trace of life on earth — for preparing death; rich countries spend what would be sufficient to guarantee the survival and to raise the standard of living of all the poor of the world, of those who are hungry, sick, oppressed. In such a situation, only an inspiration that comes from beyond our egoism, our lack of open-mindedness, will be able to introduce in our society a new force encouraging us to go against the stream, in order to defy the wheels of terror and exploitation.

So it is very important for each one of us to find, under the guidance of such competent masters, the light of a prophetical orientation that will make us depart from the commonplaces of 'good sense', which are often simply the expression of a situation that favours those who already enjoy a certain level of welfare and that asks the poor to resign themselves to accept what the rich will let them have.

This is not only important for us, it is for everybody, for it is the whole world that expects the Christians, and all believers, to show they have the strength to react, in the name of a transcendent call, against the violence of weapons and, even worse, against the violence of minds.

So I thank you all, you who have accepted to come and teach us; I thank you all, you who have come in such large numbers to hear these teachings and renew your decision to work for peace. We are all entrusted with a token for the peace of the world, for the responsability of the Christian community. It is up to us not to fail to achieve this task, with the blessing of the Lord and the intercession of the blessed Virgin Mary, the Queen of Peace.

Mgr. Paul Schruers
THE CALL OF THE BIBLICAL MESSAGE

On the one hand, when I read the Bible, I am, as a Christian, confronted in a specific way with the problems of peace. On the other hand, when working for peace and having to deal with the problems of this commitment, I discover new lights in the Bible.

The call of the biblical message

The first principle of the Bible is the historical and cosmological principle: God is love in Jesus Christ. In this light, the world is considered as a free creation of the love of God. But how can God be the God of the Alliance, the God of love for humanity and creation if we organize or prepare the destruction of the world?

The second principle of the Bible is the anthropological principle: «Whenever you did this for one of the least of important of these brothers of mine, you did it for me». Every person is loved by God and we could therefore say that he is absolute-with-God and unique. Even in the enemy, I discover the face of God. But how can one, with this man of Hiroshima, the eternal man, be ready for a war with such consequences?

The third principle of the Bible is the sociological principle: «In Jesus Christ, all are united: Jews and pagans, free men and slaves». We are called to be united in his name. But how can we then possibly replace the unity of love by the balance of distrust?

We can say that peace in a leitmotiv of the biblical revelation.

The experience of commitment to peace requires a 'spirituality'

As a militant working for peace, I have come to wonder how I can defend the values that might be questioned by the 'opponent'. The Bible tells me that true values cannot be destroyed.

There is an evangelical way to defend our values: a trust in God, one's own conversion, the testimony of the suffering servant, a trust in principle in every human being, in order to liberate one's soul. On the other hand, every form of violence darkens the true values in the eyes of others in our own lives.

As a militant working for peace, I can feel the danger of aggression and bitterness in my own heart and I also realize that the source of conflict lives inside the heart of humanity. The Bible makes me understand that peace also involves a personal and communal aspect and that ultimately, all peace is a gift of God.

As a militant working for peace, I experience despair and helplessness. But has the Bible not been written in such situations, on the basis of similar experiences? Are we not to enter glory through and experience of humiliation and crucifixion? Must we not sometimes pray with a cry of distress that is at the same time a sign of trust in the blessing of God? Does the Bible not tell us that every sign of love definitively belongs to the history of salvation, as love is always the sign of hope? So our responsability is not lessened. On the contrary, as Moltmann says, the word of the promise is a call to make, together with God, our own history.

Bernard Cardinal Alfrink
PRAYER, STUDY, ACTION

One of the fundamental goals of our Pax Christi move-ment has been, right from the beginning, to raise Christian consciousness, to perceive the flagrant discrepancy between war — modern war in particular — and the message of the Lord in the Gospel: he promises a Kingdom of justice, love and peace and asks his disciples to do their utmost in order to promote the accomplishment of such a Kingdom.

Through thorough study and work on these ideas, Pax Christi formulated, under the presidency of Cardinal Feltin, a programme that still is, in fact, the basis for the movement: prayer, study, action. These three elements are linked with each other and, together, they make up its basis and its frame-work.

By 'prayer' we do not only mean supplication, but also the inspiration that supports our enthusiasm, our reflection, the motives we have to undertake (and especially to pursue) this work on the basis of our Christian conviction. The fundamental question is to know how we try to achieve the mission Christ has entrusted us with — to love our neighbour and to be supportive of our fellow human beings — how we can contribute to pro-moting a climate that will make it possible to achieve, in the world we are living in, the peace of Christ, Pax Christi.

Mentalities, ways of thinking and of seeing things must be changed. One must face reality, and realize that modern weapons do not guarantee any security and even cause a situation of increasing insecurity. Changing mentalities also means accepting and supporting outbreaks of concern and alarm in many parts of the world, protests and demonstrations, which are sometimes unbalanced and, unfortunately, sometimes violent.

Has the time not come for Christians to commit themselves more directly to searching for new concepts of security?

It is clear that for the moment, the opposition (including military opposition) between East and West is an obstacle for the future of Europe and threatens to destroy it. The arms race will never stop by itself. It will only stop if the new generation makes it a duty to carry out some creative research work based on the Gospel, departing from the conviction that the balance of military forces is the only way to guarantee security and peace.

We will have to pursue this work and look for new ways. We cannot just take note of facts and data at an abstract level or in a spirit of neutrality. We must face the consequences and have the courage to give up thoughts or attitudes that have become questionable or are even no longer valid. As Christians especially, we have the duty to distinguish the real situation instead of hiding from reality, to open our eyes and to encourage our fellow-citizens of the world to work together in order to fulfil the conditions that will allow humanity to survive. The Gospel offers us an orientation, a vision that determines our concrete choices and responsabilities.

One can expect a Christian to choose the side of the weak, without any personal benefit and without any preference for a particular class or category of people. Another element of this Christian vision probably consists in the dimension of hope: this dimension makes us look ahead. According to Moltmann, what distinguishes us as Christians is neither our faith nor charity, but Christian hope, based on our faith and on the message of the Gospel.

Real peace is more than the mere absence of the clashing of weapons. Ultimately, peace means a situation in which human happiness would be achieved during our existence on earth. That is exactly what peace — shalom — means in the biblical sense, this concept is very important in the promises of salvation in the old and the new Testament. We often forget it is not only a promise, but also a mission. As Christians, we not only bear and announce a promise. We also bear a mission. As Christians we have a responsibility in achieving this peace, this peace of the world, in the broadest sense of the word. Both as a community of Christians and as individual Christians. That is the message of the beatitude of the Lord: 'Beati pacifici'. In the universal extension of our horizon, this beatitude has also acquired a broader interpretation. Today, we cannot be satisfied with peace in our own family, in the small community of our own group, in our own village, in our own town, in our own country. And we have to be aware of our mission, which is to take part in achieving peace for the whole of humanity in the broadest meaning which the idea of peace, of world peace, has today.

While this responsibility applies to everyone, it is especially the duty of Christians to work for peace. The Gospel of Jesus Christ is a message of peace. The Church is entrusted with announcing this message of the Lord to the whole of humanity. In the Gospel, peace between humanity and God is closely linked with peace among humans. The faith of Christians in peace must not be exclusively oriented towards the hereafter. In our times, loving our neighbour means to be ready to dedicate time and energy to others, to keep part of ourselves available for the problems that assail us from the outside. I think we also give proof of a real Christian spirit if we believe, with confidence and hope, that we are given the opportunity of contributing to achieving a new world that is taking shape progressively and the outline of which we shall only see more clearly later on.

Pastoral work will play an essential role in this awareness and this orientation towards the future, by giving the problems related to peace a central position in liturgy and preaching, as well as in catechesis for the youth and adults.

Pope John shows the full importance of prayer for peace. But he does not separate prayer from action. And he makes an urgent call upon all people of good will.

In 'Pacem in Terris', he states that there are not enough people who struggle for peace and that Christians, in the first place, should join them.

Although this task is 'enormous', we have to start accomplishing it. Nobody has the right to evade it. The point is not to lose courage at seeing so much injustice and dissension in the world, but to accept the challenge of the events we are facing. We can give proof of our evangelical inspiration by 'transposing', as it were, our mission in the daily situation.

Without expecting our intervention to have immediate or spectacular consequences, we must have the courage to work for peace at every chance and stimulate others to do the same. Great peace thoughts and expectations will have to be 'cashed in' problem by problem, stage by stage, every day anew, with courageous tenacity, in spite of all disappointments and incomprehensions. Peace is the art of standing fast, of persevering, and the ability to believe that this work does make sense, even if one cannot see the results immediately. The peacemaker must help to open up ways for the future and take the risk of not being right until tomorrow.

In a certain way, Christian churches are at the basis of European culture. For centuries, Christianity has been one of the essential vectors of European development. Christianity, which is the major religion in most countries of the East as well as the West, still is the link between both blocs. Within those Christian churches (Catholic, Orthodox and Protestant or Anglican), the creative effort that has resulted in the transformation of so many nations is one of the major guarantors for the future of Europe. We hope that this creative effort will find security models beyond the military model and beyond national security. European security will be a collective security, or it will be nothing at all.

The three Popes of the post-war period (Pius XII, John XXIII and Paul IV) have spoken out many times for the defence of peace and justice, which are directly threatened by the arms race, in Europe as well as in the Third World. The Vatican statement for the U.N.O. in 1976 has remained one of the most remarkable documents: it rejects the arms race because it is an injustice, a madness and a scandal. These are three well-known biblical expressions. I believe it is especially the task of a Catholic peace movement such as Pax Christi to take an initiative and stimulate discussion on this so essential point. The question is: How can we remain silent when facing the possibility of the complete annihiliation of other peoples? Can we take upon ourselves the responsability of being involved in such an act of total destruction?

But in the first place, we have to pray for peace. St Paul says peace is a gift of the Holy Ghost, a fruit of the Holy Ghost. Which means that it is the result of the activity of the Spirit of Jesus Christ. But, when praying, we should not forget that it is not God who makes war. Man makes war, thereby neglecting the spirit of the Gospel and acting against it. We want to pray to God and ask him to stimulate man, by his blessing, to seek peace, to avoid all causes that would act against peace, to avoid hatred, distrust, egoism, imperialism, domination, hegemony, and even the wish to enjoy one's own national security. Nowadays, there can only be a communal security of the whole of humanity of the entire human race.

Prof. Dr. Edward Schillebeeckx o.p.
IN SEARCH OF THE SALVIFIC VALUE OF A POLITICAL PRAXIS OF PEACE

Theology means speaking about God the absolute which is at stake *inside* the relative, namely *in* the historical praxis of human beings, often as a matter of life and death.

Theology articulates the ultimate and transcendent dimension of a human historical praxis, because for a believer in God a concrete praxis, even when political, bears a positive or negative - at any rate a neutral - relationship to the coming of God's kingdom. Although this kingdom has to realize itself *in* this or that particular human praxis, it cannot be reduced to that praxis. This does not take away from the fact that within a given historical situation the *absolute* and *total* character of the commitment of faith can only be expressed in a *very concrete* praxis. We shall ultimately be judged on whether we have given a glass of water to a thirsty neighbour (Mt. 25, 40).

This does not imply a reduction of the christian faith, but it forms the concrete historical situation in which the faith only can take shape. Consequently, the absolute character of faith in God can manifest itself only in particular, historical and relative ways. Who wants to experience the absolute pure and undiluted, separately available as it were, will never be confronted with it. 'God's word' is accessible to us only within the horizon of our cultural, societal and material possibilities, within the historical horizon of our lives. The absolute manifests itself only in the small and big human events of every day. It is in those events that it will have to become clear how humankind's sake or cause is God's sake or cause, and, conversely, how God's cause can become the cause of humankind. It is this that the theologian wants to unravel.

The language of faith

If ever in theology there is an accumulation of pseudo-problems, this is sure to be the case when the discussion turns to 'twin concepts' like: human freedom and grace, the human and the Christian, self-liberation and justification by grace alone, or evolution and creation. Often such contrasting concepts, which indeed refer to reality, have as such been projected into reality, where as a result they become antithetical entities, which then have to be dialectically reconciled.

The ancient polemic about grace and human freedom in the Roman Catholic Church shows what an unholy mess can be the result of such a discussion. On the level of concepts and their linguistic expression 'human freedom' and 'grace' (or the approaching of the Kingdom) are indeed *thought of* as next to and succeeding one another. They are often written on one line or put into one proposition as if we were dealing with two separate realities: 'grace *and* freedom', 'the human *and* the Christian'. The question is, however, if they can be simply added up like this. Just as a free, good act *is* concretely grace (which nonetheless transcends freedom), so a Christian can rightly experience self-liberation and, for example, a political praxis of disarmament as a piece of Christian salvation, and therefore as grace. It is this that the theologian must elucidate, or on the contrary he should demonstrate that this or that political praxis leads in fact to disaster. To be sure this is not an easy task. But wasn't this the significance of Old Testament prophecy: that the prophets tested a particular political praxis of Israel by the criterion of 'Jahweh' and then proclaimed it as salvation from God or as evil and apostasy from Jahweh? Quite often they were persecuted for their judgements, and some of them were murdered; a destiny which not even Jesus of Nazareth, the prophet of eschatological salvation, was able to escape from.

The language of faith and that of empirical analysis and description refer in these utterances to one and the same reality, but one should respect the specific pertinence and formal angle of approach of these different languages, and not mix them up. Otherwise one acts like a chess-player who suddenly puts a jack of clubs on the chess-board: a senseless, absurd gesture. If, for example, a theologian studies nothing else but the causes, characteristics and internal structure of the arms race, and on these grounds reaches a political point of view, for example: 'Free the world of nuclear weapons', he is either not acting theologically, or, if he wants to continue from there, he is exploring the 'fore-field' about which he is going to say something theological. The exploration of the terrain or of the 'material object', even if this implies a theologian's dependence on other sciences, is for him a theological task in the sense that without such search his formally theological task becomes completely nonsensical, hanging in a void. But he should remember that this prior research presupposes more than a purely theological competence. If he is engaged on a study of this forefield, a theologian will first listen carefully to human experiences, above all negative experiences of contrast and suffering, and to what other sciences have to say. On this level interdisciplinarity is suitable and even indispensable. But the theologian enters formally the theological field, where his own theological competence comes into play, at the precise moment when he submits the field he has explored to a different language, to a different set of questions, approaching it from a different angle; namely when he submits it to the language of faith, to the question about salvation and doom, approaching it from the angle of acceptance or rejection of salvation from God. At that moment there is no room left for interdisciplinarity, otherwise we would get cross-eyed by trying to look at what on the one hand is called 'human' or emancipatory liberation, and on the other 'christian' or grace and justification by grace alone. Consequently there are two language games at stake. Once the material has been analysed by reason the theologian still faces the task of de-coding or deciphering it from within the faith.The material is a text to be interpreted by him according to the grammar of Christian hope, of faith in God who is the source of universal, all-embracing and definitive salvation. We are dealing in both cases with one and the same reality: a human action or a determinate political praxis, first seen from the point of view of reason, and then in the light of faith. The question for the theologian is then: can we see, in this personal or concrete practice, if not the kingdom of God, then at least an advent or approach of it? On this level the Christian or theologian has his own, inalienable word to speak, independently of all other sciences. She or he should in such case, as I have said, have first analysed very carefully the 'secular' structure and inherent logic or rationality of this praxis within the context of its very concrete situation. Otherwise a theologian does not know what he is talking about theologically, and his contribution will be beside the point, and often vitiated by ideology. In such a case answers are provided to questions that are not asked, whereas the real question is ignored. For a Christian the appeal of revelation comes from *within this* situation, here and now. So what is at stake here is indeed the *theology of a political praxis* for the sake of universal peace.

Righteousness and peace

The Old Testament links the concept of shalom or peace with that of sedaqa or righteousness. Isaiah says: «And the work of righteousness shall be peace» (Is. 32, 17) and psalm 85, «Righteousness and peace have kissed each other» (ps. 85, 10). Nevertheless, Jewish thinking about peace starts from the concrete practice among people and among nations: there is war, there are quarrels and terrorism. As a result peace must be *brought about;* people have to return back from their evil ways, «they have to make their peace with one another» (Deut. 20, 12; Joshua 9, 15; 11, 19; Is. 27, 5). The stage of peace is the earth, the earthly history of our world, where people do 'the will of God' by practising justice (1).

In the last analysis Old Testament shalom means: to be in a condition where one has got 'sufficient', both outwardly and inwardly. Hence the common daily greeting, 'shalom', meaning: 'Good luck to you' (Judges 6, 23; 19, 20). There is only peace if both objectively and subjectively we can say without any reservation: 'like this, the way it is, it is right'. Consequently we must say that 'the peace of God' consists, under the present circumstances, in an inward discontent, in a prophetical protest against the situation as it is, and which is precisely not right the way it is. For that very reason the idea of shalom is linked with the work of righteousness. The latter concept finds its context of experience in the total complex of human conduct and the good or bad consequences this has for society and for the acting individual as well. Consequently peace is concretely and historically a social process, a road taken by the nation, directed towards 'well-being' for all, fellow-citizens as well as foreigners. Peace is finally the way God himself wants to go with his people, for the liberation and well-being of all humankind.

From the fore-going it is abundantly clear that 'biblical peace' must not be identified with absence of war or with a balance of power; neither is it the same as national security or even 'human survival.'

How can all this shed light on the problems we are confronted with here and now: on the one hand the deep chasm between wealth and poverty in the North-South-axis, and on the other the arms race spiral, especially in the East-West-axis? In order not to remain vague and abstract I intend to focus my theological reflection concretely on the present-day arms race, especially on nuclear armament.

No one can confess Jesus and call upon Him as the Christ, proclaimer and anticipatory embodiment of eschatological peace and liberation, and at the same time defend nuclear weapons, for whatever respectable reasons. This is so self-evident that among christians it is beyond discussion, unless we want to make the Christian faith into a vessel of contradictions. But this does not immediately lead to the conclusion that for example the political and strategic slogan, 'Free the world of nuclear weapons and first of all our own country' must be given the status of 'Thus speaketh Jahweh' or 'the Word of God.' Unfortunately things aren't that simple. If bishops, not as political citizens, but as leaders of the Church, have something to say about this, it must in one way or another have to do with God as source of salvation and liberation for human beings.

How far, therefore, is the absolute at stake in the (proposed) peace praxis of unilateral nuclear disarmament? How far is this praxis, here and now, the obligatory, historical and concrete form of God's promise of peace which is being realised in and through human activity; a salvation which, though expressing itself *in* this concrete activity, nevertheless transcends it? The consequence of this is, that we cannot at any rate use the transcendence of salvation and of the belief in God as a pretext for an a-political attitude or political neutrality. That would mean stripping faith of its historical dimension, and therefore of its meaning, and becoming heterodox.

This theological background makes it possible to understand a particular political praxis also in its soteriological sense, namely as salvation or grace, or, on the contrary, as sin or refusal of grace. The theological question is then: how does theology provide itself with the means to discover that salvation from God in history is already taking concrete shape in conditions where it is not yet known under a Christian name of its own, for example in a praxis of nuclear disarmament? In other words, for a believer in God political praxis contains more than what can be known of it scientifically: in such a praxis salvation from God is accepted or rejected, resulting in decisive salvation or ultimate disaster, also in the religious sense.

Nevertheless the praxis as proposed for example by the peace movements of humanist, socialist and Christian inspiration is not in itself evidently *religious*. It must be taken up within theology's own light and reflected on for it to be seen in its soteriological value. The fact that political praxis is not self-evidently religious is precisely what makes the believer in God look for a theology of this concrete praxis; it makes him ask what is its value for the faith and hence for salvation; what *positive* relation it bears to the proclamation of God's kingdom. Political praxis raises the question if it does in fact bring about 'agapè', love-through-structures, love through a very determined socio-political commitment.

A non-interpreted praxis does not exist. Christians rightly interpret a particular political activity as Christian or soteriological; and they do this rightly even if for example humanists call the same praxis (non-Christian) humanistic. For we are not allowed to take a particular socio-political praxis out of its own rationality, substance and specific aims; in this sense there is no political praxis which Christians can annex for themselves, in spite of rightly experiencing, as Christians, a particular praxis as Christian. The dream, the vision, even the promise of a better human society, a society 'with a human face', belongs to the essence of the Christian gospel, which is the political message of the kingdom of a God who is concerned with humanity and who wants people, too, to be concerned with humanity. Thus Christian faith is linked up with an ethic of humanity. Although the criteria for concrete social and political action cannot be derived directly from the 'utopia' of the kingdom of God, a believer will nevertheless incorporate this ethical activity - to be judged on its own criteria - into the theological virtues of faith, hope and love. In this way a political praxis directed towards a human and livable society is for Christians indeed the *socio-political content* of *Christian hope* in terms of an *historical* praxis.

Christians can indeed experience the political and strategic slogan, 'Free the world of nuclear weapons, and first of all our own country' as a Christian demand, while non-Christians can identify themselves equally well with the slogan, though they may call it differently. It is precisely for the believer that the 'politico-social' cannot be reduced to its political and social components: there is more at stake in it. And this 'more' has to be the object of the theologian's concern, if he wants to say something distinctly theological about this political praxis and not simply repeat what has been said about it from other fields of competence, or if on the other hand he wants to avoid giving the impression of speaking as a theologian while in fact he is speaking as a political citizen.

This is an important point in the discussion, especially if we ask the bishops to adhere to a slogan. If one wishes to let the churches and their leaders speak in a meaningful way about this, a *theological* mediation will be necessary. Otherwise one lets them say something simply as political citizens, but because they also happen to be church leaders, their words are wrongly supposed to merit more weight. This would seem to me to be a dishonest procedure, which could even lead to ideological manipulation. If we resent church leaders pronouncing on marriage, family and sexuality, why should we ask them to do the same with regard to nuclear weapons? To ask Nobel prize winners in physics for a pronouncement for or against 'Humanae Vitae' is as absurd as to ask bishops to lend public approval to the Dutch Pax Christi Report, *if* it should appear that the bishops would have to do nothing else but rubber-stamp a political praxis in its own rationality; in such a case they would indeed exceed their authority. They can only speak about the 'more' in the socio-political, but this is precisely to be found in this particular political praxis, not behind it or above it. What is historically urgent is also theologically urgent.

Our first provisional conclusion from the foregoing is now clear. If a theologian wants to be able to say something about this question as a theologian, then he must be able to speak in terms of the kingdom of God and the promises of God, translated towards a political praxis. From within a belief in God I would qualify as ideological both to want to ignore the specific contribution of theological reflection on this point (according to the slogan 'Sileat theologus in munere alieno') and to want to bring the Christian gospel into discussionwithout any mediation. We can unjustly reduce human phenomena to their religious dimension, but we can also unjustly obscure and neglect the religious dimension of a political praxis.

The obscurity of any political praxis

The ethical assessment of human conduct, including the political, must also anticipate and evaluate the effects and side-effects it could have on a national and world-wide scale. In their totality the possible effects of both nuclear armament and disarmament cannot exactly be calculated by any one, not by the sciences either. This holds good also for my individual behaviour, which I nevertheless intend to be ethically good, and yet I can be obliged to act here and now in spite of that relative ignorance. Even if I am satisfied about the ethical justification of my conduct, I may well injure and harm other people unknowingly. Consequently, even if our human conduct does not have at its command a divine 'universal providence', this does not take away from the obligation to act here and now; not acting would leave us with even greater problems. But: *how* should we act? It is clear that concrete political praxis contains a good deal of obscurity from an ethical point of view.

A situation which is unclear in itself, cannot be clarified by a theologian either. This fact has considerable consequences. Theologians may say that in every political praxis salvation or doom is realized, but taking into account the unclear nature of political actions it is often impossible to *point out* clearly the elements of salvation or doom in it. Such identification in most cases remains a very precarious matter if one does not want to end up in one or other form of conservative or progressive fundamentalism. In view of the unforeseen side-effects, our good actions are often a mixture of salvation and doom. If we cannot be theologically certain that the coming of the Kingdom of God, here and now, can be identified with nuclear disarmament, on what grounds can the bishops speak about it with ministerial authority? In this phase of our analysis we consequently reach the following first conclusion (in relation to an eventual intervention of bishops in this matter) : the gospel and nuclear weapons cannot be reconciled. The Pax Christi slogan shows the closest approximation to this Christian vision. However, '...and first of all from our own country' is *a strategy* of which no one can foresee all the consequences; about this we, as bishops cannot say: 'Word of Jahweh'; we do not know. *IF* as bishops we cannot identify *this* concrete political praxis with a coming of the kingdom of God *in* this particular praxis, we have no grounds for pronouncing on it as bishops; in this case we can only speak about it as political citizens, like all other people. But such a pronouncement would have nothing to do with our episcopal authority.

Is this all we can say about it? I don't believe it is.

Extra-specific 'cognitive certainties'

In the Pastoral Constitution 'Gaudium et Spes' of Vatican II we read: 'to investigate the signs of the times and interpret them in the light of the gospel'. Further down in the text a certain differentiation is shown: '...in the light of the gospel *and of human experience*' (nr. 46). The signs of the times do not speak, they have no voice. Human beings make them speak by interpreting them.

New ethical imperatives as reactions to a situation and the historical decisions following them are hardly ever launched by philosophers, theologians, or the pastoral authority of the Church. They arise from concrete experiences, especially from negative experiences of contrast; they apparently force themselves upon us with the evidence of experience. Only afterwards we reflect on them theoretically, investigate them critically, and provide them with sufficient grounds. Consequently the Church cannot fulfil its prophetic task vis-à-vis the world and the problems of humankind and society purely from within revelation but has to listen carefully to the *'Fremdprophetie'* which challenges her from within the secular situation. If we can analyse this 'secular prophecy' we shall see that 'historical decisions' and the inventive launching of new ethical imperatives hardly ever arise from a confrontation between 'general ethical principles' and a situation which has been scientifically analysed. Most of the time they are the result of very pronounced 'negative experiences of contrast'(from such experiences Marx' vision was born). Moreover, we are often dealing here with collective and anonymous facts. Only if at one particular spot children continually die in road accidents, collective resistance will be organized. However painful the death of one child may be, it does not provoke a collective protest. We are faced with the paradoxical and yet understandable fact that it is especially anonymous *structural violence* that arouses collective resistance, precisely because in it the 'demonic' character of violence is experienced.

If we analyse the se experiences of contrast in order to discover their possible conditions, we can observe that they include a positive but implicit perspective of value, which *manifests* itself precisely in *the protesting conscience.* In the negative experiences of contrast, in particular when their grounds disappear into the anonymous, there is as it were an indirect experience of the absence of what-ought-to-be, and thus one gets a glimpse, vaguely but unmistakably, of what *should* be here and now. This experience is, of course, nothing more than the 'preface' to reflection properly. This reflection then concerns both the scientific analysis of the situation and the fundamental values of human life, already acquired and consented to in the past. But without the pre-reflexive preface of the experience of contrast which arouses a prophetic protest neither scientific nor philosophical or theological reflection would have got under way. From such experiences even new sciences may be born, as happened for example with polemology. Through such negative experiences one discovers that he is living below the level of the fundamental possibilities of his existence and that it is often the existing social structures that have forced him to live like this. In our time such experiences of contrast lead to the ethical imperative of taking very explicit socio-political decisions. In this case the sensitive productive stimulus is not to be found in the explicit and positive thematisation as such, though this remains necessary, but in the peculiar cognitive or intelligible certainty which is hidden in the experiences of contrast and which the sciences gropingly try to thematise. This show that an historical ethical decision is not a concrete *application* of *abstract* norms which are generally valid, but that it rather finds its source in the concrete experience of a threat to humanity - a source which cannot be adequately rationalized.

However, as soon as we want to say concretely, on the ground of these negative experiences, what humanity implies *positively,* we are confronted with a plurality of projects. The common element in them is solidarity in defence of a threatened humanity. But the positive articulation of what here and now should be called humane - either theoretically or in a concrete plan for socio-political action - gives rise immediately to a multiplicity of theoretical and practical projects, and it is normally impossible to say that *this* or *that* project is the most meaningful. Here we find ourself on a terrain which is precarious, opaque and problematic, but being face to face with the threat we shall have to come to some form of action all the same. All this means that the force obliging us to engage in social action ultimately rests on the *negative* character of the experience of contrast, whereas the *positive* project(or alternative project) can only be binding in as far as it participates in the absolutely binding character of the negative content of experience.

The negative consciousness of a future freedom and an increased livability is precisely the real stimulus towards socio-political action.In general, therefore, we cannot ascribe exclusive saving power to one particular political praxis and we should not anathematise other options. All the same, when dealing with the problem of nuclear weapons, opting for a deterrent strategy means confirming and strengthening the threat to humanity. In this field the cognitive certainty inherent in the collective negative experience leads to a decisive choice from the multiplicity of possible political actions and the need for unilateral nuclear disarmament forces itself upon us, especially in view of the autonomous dynamic of the spiral effect. The deterrent strategy is no more than a respite and confirms (in spite of intentions to the contrary) precisely what the collective experience of contrast is protesting against. The possession itself of nuclear weapons becomes an intolerable burden for the public conscience, so much so that some young people have been induced to commit suicide as a result of it. If moreover we consider that private citizens cannot exercise any direct influence on the decisions of other countries, but on the other hand do have a certain influence on the decisions of the authorities in their own country, I would, taking everything into account, venture to maintain that the strategic slogan 'Free the world of nuclear weapons, and first of all our own country', implies a responsible historical decision; a decision which is closer than any others to the demands of the gospel. In this light there are grounds on which bishops also can base a theologically responsible decision to back the strategic campaign with the weight of their leadership. Unilateral disarmament may break the spell. Moreover, supposing that Western Europe did not possess nuclear weapons, what 'enemy' in possession of these weapons would use them, and by doing so first turn into a desert the country he wishes to conquer? *Cui bono?* At that moment he would be as much one of the conquered as the conqueror.

In order to avoid misunderstandings I wish to clarify that the extra-scientific cognitive certainty about which I was speaking has nothing to do with an appeal to the so-called 'gesundes Volksempfinden' which would be an extremely dangerous point of view. First of all, in such a popular feeling there is normally speaking no question of these collective experiences of contrast, but rather of positive prejudices, often of a discriminatory kind, which can be easily manipulated by a dictator. These are found on a totally different, obscure level from what is meant by negative experiences of contrast and the ethos contained in them. Moreover, I maintained that even those experiences of contrast resulting in ethical protest are nothing more than a necessary 'preface', which has to be followed by scientific and philosophical analysis and reflection; though I, too, am of the opinion that purely rational analysis will never reach the degree of intelligible certainty characteristic of collective experience of contrast. The cognitive must not be identified with what can be scientifically tested, even if such testing is necessary. There are examples of things that are evident (even if this occurs only when cultures have reached a high degree of development) without the possibility of ever verifying them rationally.

The future of the Church is its presence at the future of the world

In a remarkable study about the limits of economic growth Jay W. Forrester wrote the following: «Churches should be custodians of the longest term values in a society. Those values should look beyond civilian laws and national constitutions. As custodians of the future, Churches should understand that long-term values will conflict with the short-term values and goals of man and society. Churches must have effective ways to project long-term goals into the current processes of everyday decision-making» (2). If this is true, it certainly applies to the Churches' taks vis-à-vis the threatening spiral of nuclear armament. Too often Churches identify themselves with the shortsighted opinions of secular society, while on the other hand they proclaim only post-historical, post-earthly values. This dualism often paralyses the attitude of Churches vis-à-vis a particular socio-political praxis.

In view of the mutual dependence of all countries in the world in social and economic matters responsibility for our conduct is an empty word if we should limit ourselves to immediate necessities. Ethically our conduct in Europe must confront its consequences not only for the Third World, but also for future generations. In particular when acting socially our responsibility should extend further than the limits of our own lives. One notices as a matter of fact that the distinction between good and evil and the notion of justice and injustice are being modified more and more. We can no longer be satisfied with the question: is our conduct justified here and now, in relation to the immediate future, e.g. in relation to *our* prosperity and our well-being? We are obliged to ask ourselves if it is good and responsible for a more remote future. We should ask ourselves what is the right and responsible thing to do with a view to the future of humankind in the whole world. At stake here is our responsibility for the consequences our conduct has for the whole of mankind, with whom we feel bound in solidarity. This responsibility transcends the possibilities of the individual and demands a new ordering of socio-economic and political matters.

In fact one cannot assert that human society first fixes its objectives and scale of values, and only then asks the technologist for the means to achieve those objectives. Technology itself influences the choice of the objectives; moreover technology develops from within, from within the specific logical strength that called it to life. On account of this, new and more humane objectives become possible that formerly were beyond our reach. However, because of the dialectical relationship between society and technology one cannot make a sharp distinction between technological and ethical values. Consequently the values which in fact dominate technological development need constant critical investigation and they call for self-criticism. The factual intermingling of technology with decisions already taken and with options that imply a particular and often one-sided image of man, has given rise to a confused situation. For this reason we should oppose a division of work, which is often enough proposed, according to which science and technology are assigned to the technologists as their specific field, and the elaboration of meaning and values to the religious and humanistic movements. Even if a formal distinction is possible between the technical and the ethical, they cannot be separated with such precision: both are involved in a mutual dialectical process. To be able to do something technically does not necessarily mean to be allowed to do it ethically. As Christians therefore we must take seriously the possibility of being made, in the future, into mere objects manipulated by a technological power which is moreover controlled by a small elite. On the other hand the churches should not pretend any kind of ethical superiority; they share in the uncertainties of our culture. In spite of this they will have no choice but to speak out in all humility, especially on the grounds of the cognitive force of negative experiences of contrast which provoke the human conscience to protest from within a fundamental ethical indignation. It goes without saying that protests also can be manipulated; for that reason they should be examined on their original authenticity.

Ever since the Reformation people have rightly said that the Church is steadily in need of reform. But the question is: on which point exactly are our churches ailing? It is no longer the abuses of the late Middle Ages, but the bourgeois and privatising tendencies in Christian life and in the churches. This is the field of our present-day reformation, demanded from within the gospel of faith in God's grace that justifies us gratuitously in Jesus Christ. It is precisely our bourgeois society to which the challenge of the gospel is directed, as *affirmation* (confession) *and* as *criticism*. Because faith in God is liberating and productive, it possesses also critical power, revealing our lack of freedom and lack of peace in the world. But every attempt to give a positive concretisation of final salvation or wholeness risks either resulting in human megalomania or belittling God's possibilities. Faith in God the Creator is faith in God who is pure Positivity, who is the lord of life *and* death, but only the living lord of life, who wants salvation for all men and women and not their damnation. The faith in this God does not put our action into a very determined perspective, even politically. But we are not able to fill in, in a positive manner, the final term of that perspective, to indicate in a positive manner what the complete wholeness would be like. What we can do is to use great metaphorical master-images: «*Kingdom of God*» for the final salvation and liberation of the peaceful community of all human beings; the «*resurrection of the flesh*» for the final liberation and salvation of the personal individual within this final community and 'society of saints'; and «*the new earth and the new heaven*» as the accomplished 'ecological environment' of a truly liberated freedom and of human and humane peace.

And all this we have to start with in our temporary world and society, here and now. But, divine freedom, the source of human freedom, is not exhausted in our emancipatory history of freedom. On the other hand, finite freedom must leave God in His freedom, so that our concept of liberation and salvation cannot be fixed on what we ourselves dream and desire; it must remain open for the freedom of God which is surprising because it is absolute, and which in turn ratifies our engagement for a better and more humane world. On the other hand, for Christians this particular, unknown mode of divine freedom has become visible in Jesus Christ. The merciful righteousness of God is visible in the face of Jesus the Christ; just as this same appearance of Jesus reveals us what a human being should be. In the last resort Jesus, whom we may call God's only beloved Son, is also a human being just like you or me - except that he is even more human and humane. This confirms the permanent validity of any practice of doing good and of realizing righteousness, which nevertheless is incomplete and fragmentary because it is historically limited. It confirms also that failure and suffering in and by doing good can be a means of salvation and liberation. In this case it is an experience of the real presence of God, not in the mediation of positive support and meaningfulness, but in the mediation of extreme negativity, - in a dark night of suffering for God's and humankind's sake.

The liberation and peace asked for include, thus, a liberating renewal of economic and socio-political structures as well as an inner conversion. But those two are related dialectically. An inner conversion of the heart does not automatically change the social and economic structures, and an optimal political structure does not cause automatically the inner conversion. Moreover, in many ways bad structures obstruct an authentic inner conversion. There can therefore be no inner peace detached from a social and political context. On the contrary, «the peace of God which passes all understanding», as Paul says(Phil.

4, 7), in the circumstances at present obtaining consists of *inner disquiet*. Therefore the Christian concept of salvation loses its rational significance, if there is no *positive* relationship between justification or redemption *and* our liberating political praxis in the world, or if there is no positive relationship between eschatological salvation and social, political and economic peace which needs to be built up by human efforts. Love of God and the loving solidarity of human brotherhood and sisterhood are one single, inviolable 'divine virtue'. And «he who abides in love, abides in God, and God with him» (1 John 4, 16). That transcends any of our own attempts at universal and total liberation, which at the same time can no longer be the discriminatory postponing and marginalisation of others, the poor; not just a matter of *saving souls*. The Christian spirituality of universal peace, therefore, is both political and mystical.

Naturally the Churches appeal to the person and to the conscience of the faithful, and indeed at a point which transcends strategy, although it is the point of departure of a strategy. But there are historical situations where the prophetic challenge in fact coincides with the one and only strategy, because all other possibilities have turned out to be non-viable or insufficient. Israel had the courage to accept this historical risk and where it did not listen to the admonitions of prophecy, it had to learn through bitter experience. Of this peril, too, the Bible remains a dangerous memory.

1) See A. Eliav, Shalom. Peace in Jewish Tradition, Massadah 1977; H.P. Schmidt, Shalom. Die hebräisch-christliche Provokation, in: Weltfrieden und Revolution (Hrsg. H. Bahr), Hamburg 1968, p. 185 - 235.
2) Churches at the Transition between Growth and World Equilibrium, in: Toward Global Equilibrium (Collected Papers, ed. by D.L. Meadows and D.L. Meadows), Cambridge Mass. 1976 (337 - 353), p. 348.

Prof. Dr. Richard Friedly o.p.
RISKING PEACE

People who experienced World War II may think
of «peace» merely in terms of «no more war». Others who have
experienced war may, nevertheless, be aware of the disastrous
consequences of conflict and think of peace in an altogether
positive sense - something that is achieved only when every
mechanism which engenders fear and violence has been rendered
inoperative. A call to peace, then, envisages more than the negative goal of a mere absence of war or guns being silent. It envisages a richer future for men. Peace which is no more than absence of war can be imposed by force - as we all know only too
well- and can be maintained by a police regime through the use of
fear, evil report, suspicion, calumny, state of emergency and dic-
tatorship.

We are convinced that international treaties for the
control of armaments will be ineffective as long as hate and
jealousy are not eradicated, and the dividing up of people into
«friends and enemies», or as long as those who have a vested interest in the armaments industries are not revealed for what they
are. The demobilization of armies is a small thing compared with
the mobilization of hearts, if positive peace is to be achieved. In
seeking a solution to conflicts within the family, the school, the
professional milieu, or among nations, we must therefore no longer have recourse to «crushing the enemy».

«Building peace» has implications that go far beyond the
military dimension of ensuring peace through the use of arms.
When talking of peace we shall use the bibilical term «shalom».
The word «shalom», still in fashion nowadays, is a paradoxical
concept. What we experience in daily life is not peace and shalom
but anguish, sorrow and violence, that is to say, the absence of
true peace.

So shalom is a desired but lacking reality. All around us there is war, fear, stress, sickness, hunger and famine. We are faced with the wretched state of the refugees, the suffering of the persecuted, and exploitation in every shape and form. And amid all this misery - to be found everywhere, but particularly in the developing countries - children, women and men are longing for the time when they will receive some comfort, live in better conditions, have a little more to eat, be less subject to attack of all kinds, and be treated more justly. In short, they are looking for the signs that will tell of the dawning of the messianic promise, the coming of peace and shalom into their daily lives:

> *The people who walked in darkness*
> *have seen a great light:*
> *light has dawned upon them,*
> *dwellers in a land as dark as death...*
> *For a boy has been born for us, a son given to us*
> *and he shall be called... Prince of peace (Is 9: 1-6)*

1 - SHALOM - IN THE BIBLE, THE FOUNDATION OF HOPE

It was in everyday life among Semitic peoples that the word «shalom» was most of all used: when they met, people asked each other «Shalom?» - «How are things? Are you well?» Jesus himself greeted his disciples, fellow workers and friends in this way: «Peace be with you» (Lk 24:36; Jn 20:20-21).

«Shalom» is therefore used as a greeting by persons who are interested in one another. Such an inquiry would sound artificial and unreal if they were not. Shalom does not, then, primarily describe a situation in which nations are no longer at war with one another, nor is it a kind of «peace of soul». It suggests that between two persons who greet each other by this question there is a sense of responsibility for one another.

There is therefore no possibility of this kind of peace being found amid an anonymous mass without a human face, or among women and men in a state of fear, or among masses that are motivated by fanaticism. Such a «peace» is achieved only when everyone - including members of marginalized groups (a social layer, which, in the biblical tradition, comprises widows, orphans and strangers) - can count on being protected by the law, on being fed, on being able to live in community. Peace reigns when an end has been put to situations of injustice, famine, or disruption in the community, and so on.

Love and fidelity have come together;
justice and peace join hands.
Fidelity springs up from the earth
and justice looks down from heaven.
The Lord will add prosperity
and our land shall yield its harvest (Ps 85: 11-13).

This song full of promises indicates, in a density tinged with enthusiasm, the social dimensions this «being well» and this «becoming whole» of the shalom offered by God must be in keeping with. The work for peace is being carried on whenever broken communities recover their integral unity, whenever physical or psychic bodies are at ease, whenever the judicial arbitrariness does not trigger off anymore the spiral of repressive violence and of counter-violence, whenever our threatened environment becomes again «the home of men». Such a work is borne by our hope in the peace God offers us:

He shall judge between the nations,
and shall decide for many peoples;
and they shall beat their swords into ploughshares,
and their spears into pruning hooks;
nation shall not lift up sword against
nation,
neither shall they learn war any
more. (Is 2, 4)

Or:

>*«For behold, I create new heavens*
>*and a new earth;*
>*and the former things shall not be*
>*remembered*
>*or come into mind.*
>*But be glad and rejoice for ever*
>*in that which I create:*
>*I will rejoice in Jerusalem,*
>*and be glad in my people;*
>*no more shall be heard in it the sound of weeping*
>*and the cry of distress.*
>*They shall build houses and inhabit*
>*them;*
>*they shall plant vineyards and eat*
>*their fruit.*
>*They shall not build and another*
>*inhabit;*
>*they shall not plant and another*
>*eat;*
>*They shall not labour in vain,*
>*or bear children for calamity» (Is 65, 17-18b + 19-21 +*
>*22a, 23a)*

2 - OUR MISSION AS BUILDERS OF PEACE

Unfortunately, we know from experience that personal and social conflict prevents us bringing to every encounter the openness and sense of responsibility implied in the greeting «shalom-peace». We know also that building peace depends on other factors besides the goodwill of the individual. The social conditions under which we live and work are so marked by violence that finding the road to peace seems an impossible task, and we may be tempted to give up.

Quite often, indeed, the noises that we can hear through the too thin walls of our apartments fray our nerves. In order to be able to remain competitive, we increase the rhythm of our work in the factories. Our daily programme is often so full that we sometimes abandon relations in their loneliness. Those are forms of violence. They infiltrate into our families, our neighbourhood, our professional milieu as well as into international relations. They prevent the shalom from opening out.

1 - No resignation

But, *in pursuit of this peace,* we believers do not give up, *despite national and international structures which are obstacles to peace.* We trust in the assurance given us by Christ in support of our efforts to eliminate violence, poverty and fear: *«Blessed are the peace-makers; God shall call them his sons»* (Mt 5: 9). Some may think that this beatitude has no real significance when, day after day, the TV celebrates ruthlessness on the part of its heroes and the blatant use of violence; when the pressures of everyday life make men, women and young persons feel so lonely that suicide is increasingly looked to as a means of escape; when the impoverishment of the Third World forms part of business deals on the Western financial market; when so much energy is wasted on the production and export of armaments; when those who object to military service on the basis of this beatitude are severely punished; when it becomes necessary to set up homes for battered women, and telephone services for children in trouble. But this beatitude is very relevant today, certainly for those who are committed to altering situations which involve violence, fear and conflict. From it they derive the courage to face up to opposition, misunderstandings, and other difficulties, because it proclaims the reconciliation brought about by the death of Jesus.

*But now in Christ Jesus you
who once were far off have been brought
near in the blood of Christ. For he is
our peace, who has made us both one,
and has broken down the dividing wall
of hostility, by abolishing in his flesh
the law of commandments and ordinances, that he might create in himself
one new man in place of the two, so
making peace, and might reconcile us
both to God in one body through the
cross, thereby bringing the hostility to an
end. (Ep 2, 13-16)*

2 - Because of Christ

This new reality, *reconciliation,* is entrusted to those who believe in Jesus Christ. Since, in their case, this peace has in prac- tice been realized, they have the confidence and the ability to find means of spreading this message of reconciliation and peace. Ac- tive non-violence is not an option but a duty for these «sons of God»:

*Therefore, since we are justified by faith, we have
peace with God through our Lord Jesus Christ... (Rom 5,
1)*

Or:

*Repay no one evil for evil, but
take thought for what is noble
in the sight of all. If possible, so
far as it lies with you, live at peace with all men. My
dear friends, do not seek revenge but leave a place for
divine retribution, for there is a text which reads:
Justice is mine, says the Lord, I will repay (Rom 12: 17-
19).*

This duty to spread peace determines not only a Christian's behaviour within the community but also the Christian's treatment of his «enemy», for the coming of the kingdom of God is proclaimed to all men without exception: Jesus announced it to the centurion in Capharnaum even though this Roman was the military and political enemy (Mt 8: 10-13).

3 - Mission as «hope in action»

This bold systematic attempt to abate all forms of attack in private or public life, and this refusal to make use of violence to resolve tension between persons or states, is linked in a fundamental way with «mission», the Church's duty. The ecclesial community proclaims «good news»: its vocation is to be a «sign of peace». In conflictual situations, «mission» involves the duty of finding methods of reconciliation and ways of protesting that are in keeping with mankind's desire for peace. In the unsettled social, political and religious milieu in which he lived, Jesus Christ clearly committed himself to such a policy. By his «go forth and make all nations my disciples»(Mt 28, 19) he gives us our mission as disciples and followers. He imposes on us the duty of «teaching all that I have commanded» to every community in the world. *Jesus Christ is the norm* for our life-style as builders of peace:«As thou hast sent me into the world, I have sent them into the world (Jn 17, 18). I give you a new commandment. Love one another. As I have loved you, so you are to love one another».

The missionary mentality requires us day by day, in our relations with the world, to act in such a way that our life contributes to the growth of justice and the kingdom of God in and around us. *We would be false prophets* if our appeal for peace were mere verbiage, made without due reflection.(Jer 6, 14) But, in the context of «shalom» and hope, our communities will be prophetic whenever they intervene in a critical manner in the course of events in order to make it possible for men and women to live again in a really human fashion without having to wear masks: *«for God shows no partiality». (Rom 2, 11)*

It is through our readiness for self-criticism and dialogue - dialogue between «us» and «them», between nationals and foreigners, between whites and blacks, between managers and workers, between persons from Europe and persons from the Third World - that the Church grows in the world. For «God has gathered together as one all those who in faith look upon Jesus as the author of salvation and the source of unity and peace, and has established them as the Church, so that for each and all she may be the visible sacrament of this saving unity (Lumen gentitum no. 9). This is the mission Jesus received from his Father and gave to us - the building of peace among men. (Jn 14: 27)

4 - A task beset with risks

This mission is fraught with danger. Both the Old and the New Testaments see true peace-shalom as not being limited to the pacifying of aching hearts and troubled consciences, but as requiring also that believers take part in everyday political and public life.

Charity and the ministry of reconciliation affect more than *private life* (the giving of alms may, for example, even add to the fundamental inequalities among men). Both the proclamation of the Gospel and the tackling of structures with a view to promoting shalom in every community form part of the Church's mission, and bear witness to her dynamism inspired by the hope that is hers.

This mission and action require us to learn to live with our own tendencies to aggression, through analysis of our own conflictual situations and finding a way to tone them down. As persons baptized and confirmed in the name of Jesus Christ, we have a special obligation to tackle problems together, each one giving of his best - as educator, psychologist, sociologist, social worker, legal or military expert, or whatever. Only through a joint approach, offering gleams of hope to all parties concerned, will committed radical action on our part be succesful when we confront the «powers» (Eph 6, 11-12) of this world as they manipulate men physically, socially and politically.

We know how dangerous this task of building peace is: the life of Christ tells us so. It was in such a struggle that he died - for all men, his enemies as well as his friends. But hope proved stronger, and it is under the inspiration of this interior strength of the risen Lord that we carry on with our mission for peace: *«I have told you all this so that in me you may find peace. In the world you will have trouble. But, courage! The victory is mine» (Jn 16: 33).*

But in *the context of suffering and failure that lead to the death on the cross,* one cannot place on the same level the peace of God and the human efforts for peace. The quest for peace is always achieved in the frame of this passing world and even the achievement of peace must take upon itself sin and fault. For this reason, even success in the search for peace remains provisional - and failure still does not provide evidence of the absence of God. This gives the Christian the strength that is required for the practice of peace, but also takes away illusion of peace.

3 - MORE AGGRESSIVENESS AMONG CHRISTIANS WHO CALL THEMSELVES «ORTHODOX»?

Working for peace, then, has nothing to do with feverish activity or injudicious proselytism. Nor is it restricted to believers. Indeed, it would seem that the claim made by Christians (so often heard in the liturgy, in preaching and in catechesis) - that, besides appealing for peace, they are also very actively engaged in contructing a more harmonious world - is open to question. In-depth inquiries into the outlook and behaviour of Christians and non-Christians vis-à-vis social problems would lead to serious reservations about the actual contributions which Christians make to the cause of peace.

In those surveys, the respondents had to answer questions on topics such as military service, nuclear arms, the death penalty, the obligation to make some contribution as a world citizen, the need for a research institute to promote peace. The respondents were also asked to state where they saw themselves in the matter of religious commitment, on a scale that ranged over a dozen or so possibilities from «convinced believer» to «regular practiser» or «non-believer».

Surveys carried out during the 1960s and the 1970s in Canada, and the USA, among various élites (church dignitaries, business managers, university students, etc.), revealed a striking contradiction among Christians in respect of Christ's message of love and peace. Christians who call themselves orthodox were more inclined to war than the non-Christians were; Christians who claimed to be strict in matters of faith were much more ready to inflict punishment than those who said they were not very keen about doctrine; Catholics were more in favour of nuclear arms than were Protestants, and the latter, in their turn, were more in favour of such weapons that non-believers. In all the groups studies, practising Christians showed a much more clear-cut tendency than non-practising Christians to accept military power as a means of resolving conflict. Those who prided themselves on having a religious view of the world were less interested in a world community than those who said their outlook was not very religious.

We do not intend to discuss here what lay behind these discoveries. We give a few hypotheses that were put forward in an attempt to explain this contradiction between the preaching of active love in Christian churches and the harsh attitudes of practising Christians in situations of social conflict: (i) collusion between Church and political authorities, (ii) the fixed dogmatic nature of the formulations of the original Gospel message, (iii) the intolerance inherent in a prophetic religion, (iv) the fact of referring to a god who is severe and punishes.

We shall not discuss the validity or otherwise of these suggested explanations, but it does seem that one may conclude from the replies to the questionnaires that Christians are marked by points of view and behaviour which indicate a tendency towards severity, authoritarianism and censoriousness, a tendency to defend the established order, to suppress differences («We must oppose evil»), and a fear of conflict. If such conclusions are taken seriously, then appeals for peace emanating from ecclesial circles will only be credible in so far as ecclesial communities become communities undergoing a process of real conversion - conversion in the matter of doctrinal prejudices, moralizing aggressiveness, and misuse of hierarchical power.

4 - EVANGELICAL METHODS OF PROMOTING PEACE

The Churches will be able to create a climate of trust conducive to a reduction in the level of fear, violence and suffering, at local and world level, only if Christians free themselves from stress and agitation. But, apart from this moral challenge, have we, as Christians, anything else to offer by way of technique and method which will promote peace?

In this context, we point among other things to three practical lines of action.

1 - Always take the initiative

Jesus asks us to always take the initiative in the matter of reconciliation, even when we are in the right and the other party is at fault. «*If, when you are bringing your gift to the altar you suddenly remember that your brother has a grievance against you, leave your gift where it is before the altar. First go and make peace with your brother, and only then come back and offer your gift*» *(Mt 5: 23-24)*. Because «*that one of you who is faultless shall throw the first stone*» *(Jn 8: 7)*.

How can we ourselves take the initiative in situations such as the following:

when communication *between husband and wife* becomes difficult because of, for instance, professional commitment in a society based on competition, lack of money, sexual problems?

when misunderstandings *between parents and children* are such that practically any gesture of true reconciliation is impossible?

when, *in the parish,* members are divided and at loggerheads over liturgical questions?

when *a State* has to make the first step in diplomacy in respect of some enemy State or should begin by responsible and effective disarmament?

And if these efforts at reconciliation should fail (at family, parish or state level), what lines of action would tie in most closely with such a desire for reconciliation?

2 - *Always give another chance to the other party*

All men and women bear signs of the presence of grace as well as of sin. We are, so to speak, points where positive dispositions and destructive tendencies intersect. That is why, in any encounter between persons, or even nations, there should be a bias in favour of the other party. When this is so, it is an encouragement to the other party to take the initiative instead of remaining tied down to what is past. The word «pardon» implies just this situation - at least in the perspective of the Sermon on the Mount (Mt 7: 1-5; cf. also 18: 21-22). Pardon *cannot, moreover, be confined to the realm of a penitential liturgy or private confession.* Linked with it is the quest for effective methods for helping persons and groups to re-establish contact with one another (for example, methods of negotiation, arbitration, discussion techniques, pursuit of real compromise).

Ancient forms of peace work could here be again of great use for the individual and the parish when it is a matter of giving the other a real chance: let us think of common *fast,* of supportive *prayer* of intercession, of *renouncing sleep*, or of a meditative and quiet pilgrimage. Those ascetic practices are not a sort of prowess (Mt 6, 1-17), but a means to purify our deep intentions, to clarify the selfish mind that always wants to be right, to keep away any blindness caused by our own self, and to prepare the radical gift to the benevolent God.

3 - *Do not stress being right*

What is really important is that we live in a positive and «constructive» fashion inside the human and Christian community - not the consciousness of knowing we are in the right or in a position to crush the other party by arguments: «*Let us therefore cease judging one another, but rather make this simple judgement: that no obstacle or stumbling block be placed in a brother's way... Let us pursue the things that make for peace and build up the common life*» *(Rom 14: 13, 19)* The decisive criteria are not to be found in the world of ideas but in the world of persons: truth, while being as hard as a diamond, is as delicate as a flower. The priority attributed to «constructive» community behaviour means that action by one who is conscious of «possessing the truth» is practically valueless. Out of all this arises a mass of questions in which Christians, in and with the active support of people around them, are able to contribute towards the attainment of a peace that is positive and realistic:

How, for example, can architects build the kind of apartments and houses that will lessen tension and give fewer grounds for recrimination among persons who live in them?

How can the tempo of professional, scholastic or domestic life be altered with a view to reducing the stress, nervous depression and suicides it now leads to?

What can communes and parishes do, by provision of recreational spaces and richer leisure pursuits, to bring about better understanding between persons?

What practical neighbourly help can be given to alleviate the suffering from overwork and fatigue now afflicting many mothers and fathers of families?

What juridical steps are urgently needed if we really wish to make foreign Christians welcome and full members of our ecclesial communities?

What form should thoughtful hospitality and active tolerance take vis-à-vis refugees, foreigners and immigrant workers?

How are we to uncover the craving for power and the various forms of tyranny to be found in councils and groups in the parish, in politics, and in military circles?

How can we alleviate the material and moral worries of families with one of their members locked up for some felony, or for being a conscientious objector?

How can we get as much money spent on research into the causes of aggressiveness, in the hope of reducing national and international conflict, as is now spent on armaments - sums that run into milliards of dollars?

How are we to lessen the aggressiveness which surveys reveal as existing among practising Christians (cf. point 3) in order to ensure that the scruples of conscientious objectors are considered with the seriousness that is dedicated to the justification of national resistance to attack from outside, that is, to the establishing of the conditions for a just war?

These and similar questions evoke life-styles which cannot, perhaps, be promoted by hierarchies which are purely masculine. For, in such hierarchies, there is often a lack of attitudes or values such as vulnerability, openness to others, real sympathy, true sensitiveness, deep compassion, unshakeable courage. The pursuit of candid cooperation between men and women could result in a much greater sense of fraternity in interpersonal relations, and this would be something to offer to civil society. What is the point of being right or of possessing the truth, if this means utter disaster to the brother or sister «for whom Christ died?» (1 Cor. 8: 11).

5 - THE PRACTICE OF PEACE AND ITS MEANING

These traditional approaches to peace - taking the initiative, granting others another chance, and being constructive - apart from enabling us to get along within our communities, also involve active tolerance of the party with whom we find ourselves in conflict. The actual ecclesial community thus becomes a forum for resolving conflict: peace and shalom appear as attainable, or are already present in embryo, and can be imitated by others. Our reconciliation with God - made possible by Christ - becomes all the more manifest when groups and persons are reconciled and when peace is established between them. Conflict is no longer brushed to one side or passed over in silence. Instead, through this very conflict, we work out new models of behaviour and of mutual understanding, just as, for example, the Apostles did in the conflict which had Christians of Jewish origin opposed to Christians of Greek origin, at the meeting in Jerusalem (Acts 15) or during the disagreement between St Paul and St Peter at Antioch (Gal 2: 11-21).

Mere proclamation of peace by church representatives is not enough. They must also work at uncovering and toning down the bellicose psychic and spiritual inclinations to be found within their own persons, within their own communities, and even in their less immediate surroundings. This is the road of penitence. The will to repent, in either the private or the public sphere, necessarily implies the taking of practical measures at every level. It includes, among other things, readiness to spend money to enable research workers, in various scientific domains concerned with violence, and practitioners, with experience of the means of social change, to contribute towards translating what is said about peace into the practice of peace at national and international level.

There is a price to be paid by those who decide to accept the invitation to work for peace. It is but one of the many aspects of the serious nature of Jesus' invitation to follow him. «*You must not think that I have come to bring peace to the earth: I have not come to bring peace but a sword*» *(Mt 10: 34)* Those words were not meant to justify war: they refered to the costly and clear decision to be made once the kingdom of God came our way. The fact of our being reconciled by the death and resurrection of Christ stops us Christians from accepting war as a necessary evil. We are not justified in joining in the arms race, even when we see the enemy committed to it. Organized national defence or armed resistance to collective aggression is legitimate under certain conditions (Gaudium et Spes, no. 79, par. 4) but such activities depend on an ethic of disaster, in situations where every other non-violent means has failed to resolve the conflict.

6 - MEDITATION AS AN AID TO PEACE

Many moral and natural sciences help the cause of peace. As Christians, we should be competent in them - not all of us in each of them, but as a community. Contemplative meditation has its own specific religious contribution to make to that cause. It can help to bring peace to men's hearts and into interpersonal relationships. The meditative approach - by its openness to transcendent reality - frees the superficial everyday «self» from the roles it thinks itself obliged to play, roles which are often distorted by the «friends-enemies» schema. This is possible because knowledge obtained in meditation does not function like rational knowledge, which advances by objective technical analysis. Meditation knows men and things through an inner, loving sharing. The unfriendly division into «us here» and «those there» is eliminated, and the way lies open to a cooperative encounter. Factors that separate men - such as character, race, social position, or religious loyalties - are toned down.

1 - Training for peace and meditation

In meditation, the self, through which each person, even the «enemy» is bound to God, is strengthened in its deepest roots and feels so secure that it is delivered from fear, especially the fear of being ridiculed or maligned on account of its concern for peace. The sense of personal security thus acquired enables the person to work untiringly in the interests of a new policy of security. And this policy will be more solid and more resistant than one based exclusively on armaments. Reliance on armaments stems, in fact, from fear. A «balance of arms» is dangerous and is a threat to peace as long as it is not firmly supported by a «balance of trust». Our aim is a balance between «armed service of peace» and «non-armed service of peace», between the mobilization of arms and the mobilization of hearts.

In this quest for ways of guaranteeing psychological and political security, the spiritual masters of every period could become increasingly relevant. With an astonishing sureness of judgement and with lucid realism they have, in fact, perceived the close link between *violence, fear and unbridled sexuality* on the one hand, and non-violence, security and integrated sexuality on the other. The latter qualities would be associated with what they call a *chaste attitude.* Awareness in this field would create in every kind of community - family, groups of families, religious communities, priestly communities, professional circles, associations, parishes, trade unions - the social climate which is needed for the bold approach of *«fraternal correction»* (cf Mt 18: 15-17 and Lk 17: 3—4) to become a way of lessening conflict and of advancing the cause of peace.

2 - Mysticism and politics

This is not the place to talk about the different Christian and non Christian methods of a meditation process. But each one of these methods of contemplation has its own way of deepening the close link between personal experience and practical consequences, between mysticism and politics. Nicolas de Flue, for instance, was so purified by his contemplation of the mystery of the Passion, of the Eucharist and of the trinitarian mystery, that he became a very important political adviser. Strengthened by his interiority and having become mature enough through his political activiy in the service of the fatherland, this «lover of peace» could in a clear and trustworthy manner take a position against the service of the Swiss mercenaries and against the increase in atrocities of war, brigandage and torture. The corporal works of mercy in his view of meditation - to give food to the hungry, to give drink to the thirsty, to welcome the strangers, to clothe the naked, to free the emprisoned, to bury the dead - are not only acts of personal sanctification, but also serious invitations to change the conditions of national and international life, which, everywhere, always give birth to similar needs.

And so, peace education will acquire, from the progress of meditation, a *spirituality* and a method that will allow this promise to be achieved: *There is neither Jew nor Greek, there is neither slave nor free, there is neither male nor female; for you are all one in Christ Jesus. (Ga 3, 28).*

7 - *THE CHURCH A LABORATORY OF PEACE*

Love of the enemy, then, ceases to be merely a topic for preaching and liturgy. Church communities must venture more and more to bestir themselves and to undergo a kind of apprenticeship in order to stimulate definite commitment to the cause of peace among small life-groups and working-groups. Such a school of peace does not take refuge behind blind patriotism, but sets about systematically reducing conflicts and rendering the arms race superfluous.

Obviously, global perspectives on peace can only be realized at the level of local groups. The example of a Mahatma Gandhi, or a Martin Luther King, or an Oscar Romero, or many other Christians, are good illustrations of this realism. The quest for «shalom» succeeds and becomes reality, not through discussion of principles but through concrete acts, however insignificant. In that sense the ecclesial community is an experimental community and a pilgrim community. It is a multinational laboratory where:

- reflexes stemming from fear are overcome
- extra information compensates for distorted reality
- alternative styles of community life are worked out for the family and for the religious life
- emphasis is laid on learning to dialogue and to analyse things with a critical eye
- the dangers to peace are, through prayer and the Eucharist, put into the hands of God.

That is how Christians make a small but very real contribution to this very complex search after peace.

Prof. Dr. Enrico Chiavacci
PEACE SPIRITUALITY, DISARMAMENT AND SECURITY

1. Biblical starting-point

The gift of the resurrected Christi is peace. The greeting to the disciples, on the evening of the resurrection, cannot be interpreted as a simple salutation. There is a strict relationship between Jn 20, 19-20 and Jn 14, 27; 17, 21. So peace is a relational whole, on the trinitarian model; peace is possible through the spirit, i.e. the internal logic of the trinitarian relationship, charity as a total gift of oneself to the other. And precisely that spirit is given to us through the resurrection.

The entire prophetical announcement regards peace as the implementation of the will of God in his people and — at the limit — in the human family. Remember that *the justice of God — the only one to be dealt with in the Scriptures — is always the justice done to the poor,* and that the poor are the oppressed or those who are defenceless against a potential oppression (such as the alien, the widow, the orphan). *The justice of God is a radically biased justice.*

Jesus Christi places himself in the direct line of the prophets — as appears in Lk 4 and the Beatitudes — and, through the trinitarian revelation, gives it a new dimension (without limits: love the way I have loved you) and a final motivation (God is charity and gift of oneself).

2. An attempt to define peace according to the 2nd Vatican Council

I suggest a definition of *peace* on earth, as the order wanted by God, consisting of two elements, a positive and a negative one:

- *The end of every oppressive state of things*, of every form of physical and psychological oppression of man against man.

- *Universal brotherhood*, where *brotherhood* is the full gift of oneself, the recognition of the other — no matter who, even the smallest, even the most wicked — as valuable to me; and *universal* excludes any kind of prejudice and particularly — in this context — of prejudice caused by borders between countries or political blocs.

So the spirituality of peace is based on a double direction which God wants for the human family. *The powers of darkness* (absolute evil) oppose this progress of mankind and must be overcome. The spirituality of peace is the inner certainty that this task has been entrusted to everyone of us, as believers — «As thou didst send me into the world, so I have sent them into the world» — and that consequently, the ultimate meaning of our existence must be understood as a task within the history of man and for man in history. Man is the way of the Church. The peace to which are entire existence is committed is at the same time 'figura et effectus' of the peace of Christ: it comes from the Spirit that was given to us and must shape itself on the final model of the celestial Jerusalem. For mankind, as well as for each individual person, there is no other goal but this Jerusalem.

3. *The concept of security*

People often say that peace is a beautiful thing, but always in a context of security. Now the justification of the arms race is security. But whose security? The security of *our* country, of *our* towns? But if one considers the security of the human family, then armaments — especially nuclear weapons — represent the highest level of insecurity and even the assurance of death and utter devastation.

Merely to consider using nuclear weapons creates the moral possibility of perpetuating massacres, endless disasters for humanity now and in the future just to preserve my own security. Therefore, we must refuse the euromissiles not because they are dangerous for Europe, but because they are dangerous for humanity. There is a standard limit to legitimate defence, which has been acknowledged by the entire traditional moral theology; the use of nuclear weapons is, on principle, always far beyond this limit.

The economic dimensions of the present arms race are already the assurance of death, of tragedies beyond what one can imagine, in the entire South (in the meaning expressed in the *Brandt Report*) particularly in the very poor countries. In the North, the average expectation of life is higher that 70 years; in the South, it is lower than 55 years; all the children of the North reach the age of 10; in the South, only a minority of them do. Famine, diseases due to insufficient food or medical care, dispersion of families, several millions of poor dying of starvation every year: all that is war indeed, *a violent lack of peace, foreseen, wanted or maintained by the political and economic powers of the North.*

Now — and especially since Mr Reagan was elected — aid and assistance to the South have been reduced and exploitation has been increased, in oder to allow an increase in the economic and technological resources used for armaments. And they call all that 'defending peace'. Jeremiah's reproach is really topical now, more than it has ever been before: «*For from the least to the greatest of them, every one is greedy for unjust gains; and from prophet to priest, every one deals falsely. They have healed the wound of my people lightly, saying 'Peace, peace', when there is no peace*». (Jer 6, 13-14)

It is clear now that only disarmament meets with the Christian concept of peace and security. Any other choice is incompatible with our faith: to consider oneself as committed in that direction is neither a good thing, nor simply a possibility for a Christian. *It is an absolute duty;* it is — in this tragic moment of human history — the inescapable consequence of paschal faith.

4. Spirituality and politics

As we saw, a spirituality of peace is a profound attitude which consists in considering ourselves as engaged in history. In history, there is a *mystery*: the spirit of God is working within it. *When talking about the spirituality of peace, we must avoid a twofold temptation, which I shall call the eschatological temptation and the privatizing temptation.*

The eschatological temptation

Peace is the gift of the resurrected Christ. It will be the final gift of a new heaven and a new earth. The desperation and frustration resulting from the extreme difficulty of being *peacemakers* can find consolation in the hope of the celestial Jerusalem and, besides that, the justification of escapism from a commitment which seems utopian. *The spirituality of peace is, on the contrary, the spirituality of historical commitment.* And this is precisely the message of the entire 'Gaudium et Spes' Constitution, which is expressed in conclusion no. 93.

The privatizing temptation

We are confronted with power every day. And power as a goal is the power of the darkness: 'Tu solus dominus'. This is why we may be tempted to refuse any structural commitment to movements which attempt to change the course of history. To find peace in my own spirit, to bring peace into immediate personal relationships: that is where the temptation lies. We refuse a relationship which is simultaneously personal (i.e. between persons, the subjects of history) and mediate (through the political, economic and social structures).

Now it must be said very clearly that this refusal of the political is a refusal of history.

Now that the conditioning-power of structures has acquired incomparable importance, *the spirituality of peace must confront these forces — the really strong forces of darkness — must make a commitment to disrupt them, must cooperate with all people of good will to consider and create an alternative. Otherwise, we are dealing with biography, not with history.*

Assistance to the poor and the oppressed of the earth is a totally necessary and urgent task but if it is limited to its own horizon as charity, it is not yet a commitment to peace.

I think that, quite often, the fact of returning — or fleeing — into privacy is rationalized or justified by the devilish argumentation of power; but in reality, it means avoiding the aridity of more institutional action, the risk of a choice without previous certainty and the hazards of a task which, at first sight, is hopeless.

A true spirituality of peace can well see and live the moment of privacy, but always within the overall framework of human history now and in the future. Without hope, and even contrary to any hope, without faith in the presence of God in history without a charity that goes beyond the satisfaction of personal relationships, into space and time — without all this, biblical peace does not make sense anymore.

Briefly, if we accept the biblical concept of peace — the task which the Lord has entrusted to us — then we must today accept the political.

Mary Evelyn Jegen s.n.d.
CHRISTIAN SPIRITUALITY, DISARMAMENT AND SECURITY

Before attempting to link peace spirituality with disarmament and security, it will be useful to propose a working definition of spirituality. Spirituality has been aptly called «theology in walking shoes.» This is an apt description because it expresses two aspects of spirituality. First, it reminds us that while theology can, and sometimes does remain an academic exercise, spirituality for good or ill attempts to integrate an understanding of the things of God with the experience of daily life. Second, calling spirituality «theology in walking shoes» reminds us that spirituality is not something static, finished once and for all, but it is a journey, a reality tending in some direction.

Each of us has some kind of spirituality, that is, some attempt to integrate in some coherent fashion the central mysteries of our faith with our personal and social experiences. The mystery of faith with which we are particularly concerned here is God's gift of peace. The root meaning of peace, from the Hebrew *shalom*, is wholeness. Originally peace meant physical integrity. This was later extended to mean integral human development. It is interesting to note in the Gospel of John that Our Lord promised us peace as a gift on the night before He died, and that in all the post-resurrection appearances his greeting his «shalom». It is quite clear that peace is his gift. Scripture scholars tell us that in his greeting «shalom» Our Lord was conveying the idea that he had fulfilled a pledge, a commitment. It is as though He were saying to us, «I have been faithful to the struggle to the end, and now I share my prize, my integrity, my peace.»

Peace is also a task. The task dimension is expressed most clearly in the Beatitudes, and here it is worth noting that «Blessed are the peacemakers» is the only one of the eight Beatitudes to which is attached the promise, «*for they will be known as children of God.*» Jesus tells us that when we are about the work of making peace the Father recognizes us as bearing his image, as his own children.

The quality of our spirituality will be directly related to the quality of our prayer. Prayer can be most simply described as paying attention to God in whom we live and move and have our being. If we are attentive to God who fills the universe by his essence, presence, and power, who lives in us, and whose Spirit toils in us and loves in us, we will be drawn to be attentive also to those dearest to Him, that is, to the joys and hopes, the griefs and anxieties of the men, women, and children of our time. Like Jesus, we will be drawn especially to those who are poor or in any way afflicted.

A spirituality of peacemaking which is attentive in this way will enable us to manage the tensions inherent in struggling for peace and justice in a world wounded not only by personal sin, but also by sinful attitudes and practices expressed through social, economic, and political institutions.

Our struggle for disarmament brings our peace spirituality to bear on perhaps the most stubborn and threatening evil institution of our time, the arms race. There are several characteristics of the arms race that require careful attention. Our current arms race has gone on at an accelerating pace for over thirty-five years, an entire generation. That means that many adults have lived their entire lives in a political and social climate of armed hostility. Much has been written on the economic and social cost of the arms race; less has been written on a dimension that may be far more significant, namely, the psychological effects of living in a situation of mutually assured destruction.

In confusing and even obliterating the distinction between combatant and noncombatant, between defense and attack, in looking upon civilians within range of military targets as so much «collateral damage», nuclear weapons policy has perhaps worked its greatest mischief in corrupting a vision of the splendor and value of the human person.

It is one thing to grow up trained to perceive others as enemies; it is quite another to be a citizen of a nation armed against another nation for mutually assured destruction. This balance of terror is, I believe, itself a terrible moral evil and spiritually destructive. We need to ponder whether it is possible to acquiesce over a long period of time in a policy that tolerates planning for massive slaughter without losing touch with the springs of love and trust on which human development depends. The arms race is itself brutalizing.

We have been indoctrinated with the notion that some kind of weaponry of mass destruction is an unfortunate but necessary means to security. Security is without question a genuine human need, and providing for it is one of the chief reasons for establishing any society. It is a dangerous error, however, to equate security with defense and an even greater error to equate it with armed defense. Whether on the personal or social level, defense, or fending off someone hostile, is only one dimension of security. The principal activities which provide true security are those which nurture the development of persons and groups, those which provide for the common good by assuring a just society. Further, since we are concerned with a Christian spirituality, we must pay close attention to the teaching of Jesus to love our enemies, to do good to those who hurt us.

Much of what passes for action on behalf of security is in fact done to satisfy less noble ends. The enormous cynicism of many people concerning government policies comes from a recognition that the arms race is motivated much less by a noble desire to defend than by base motives of greed. To spend billions of dollars annually for weaponry which is supposed to defend by threat alone would be silly if it were not so dangerous. In point of fact, by a combination of dishonesty and error of judgment the two nations which lead the arms race have made themselves international bullies and terrorists, holding not only each other, but the rest of the world hostage. No amount of dressing up the situation in scientific and political sophistry can conceal this brutal fact.

In the face of this situation, what will be the characteristics of a spirituality of peacemaking? It must begin in an act of repentance. Without making judgments about personal or individual guilt, we need to make an honest evaluation of the arms race and acknowledge it as morally intolerable. Once this judgment is made, it is clear that the arms race is propelled not only by those who manipulate it for gain, but equally seriously, by those who allow it to continue through indifference.

The next step, then, must be a commitment to a long and arduous struggle to rid the world of the scourge of the arms race. If this will to disarmament is to be more than a vague aspiration it must engage the forces which produced and maintain the arms race. In this struggle a Christian spirituality will have its own distinctive contribution, on condition that there are in fact Christians who embody that spirituality, for spirituality, it must be remembered, is not a body of doctrine, but the application of religious understanding to actual life.

Christians should first of all find their security not in political or military might, but in the way of God revealed in Jesus. It is unmistakeably clear in the Gospel that Jesus gathered disciples, and taught them by his words, but especially by his life, how to live most fully by a fundamental disposition to love others at one's own expense. He himself did this in a situation of conflict, a conflict caused by his unswerving solidarity with the poor and oppressed. He so antagonized the religious and political leaders of his day that they conspired successfully to kill him.

We have Jesus' own perspective on his life and death as recorded in the Gospel of John, «The father loves me, because I lay down my life in order to take it up again. No one takes it from me; I lay it down of my own free will, and as it is in my power to lay it down, so it is in my power to take it up again; and this is the command I have been given by my Father.» (John 10: 17-18)

The majority of the contemporaries of Jesus responded to this words and life with intellectual confusion and moral indifference. John tells us, «Many said, 'He is possessed, he is raving; why bother to listen to him?'» The followers of Jesus, who were soon to be known as Christians, responded differently. No one has spoken for them more eloquently than St. Paul, for whom Jesus' nonviolent resistance to death was the very center of the Gospel. Paul writes. «The language of the Cross may be illogical to those who are not on the way to salvation, but those of us who are on the way see it as the power to save. As scripture says: I shall destroy the wisdom of the wise and bring to nothing all the learning of the learned. Where are the philosophers now? Where are the scribes? Where are any of our thinkers today? Do you see now how God has shown up the foolishness of human wisdom?» (1 Cor. 1: 18-20)

We are inclined to think of the Cross as the way to personal salvation, and not as a way having application to political realities. Today that fracture must be healed. Faced by the possibility, even by the probability or prospect of a nuclear holocaust, we need first of all to bring home to ourselves that the greatest devastation of such a holocaust would not be physical, that while nuclear weapons would destroy our bodies, our willingness to use them destroys our souls.

Love has become an imperative, a necessity for survival - a love that is categorical in its refusal to see others as expendable for whatever ends. It is Paul again who describes the experience of this love in terms of the mystery of the Cross.

«We are only the earthenware jars that hold this treasure, to make it clear that such an overwhelming power comes from God and not from us. We are in difficulties on all sides, but never cornered; we see no answer to our problems, but never despair; we have been persecuted, but never deserted; knocked down, but never killed; always, wherever we may be, we carry within our bodies the death of Jesus, so that the life of Jesus, too, may always be seen in our body. Indeed, while we are still alive, we are consigned to our death every day, for the sake of Jesus, so that in our mortal flesh the life of Jesus, too, may be openly shown. So death is at work in us, but life in you.» (2 Cor. 4:7-12)

Our cultural attitudes are shaped perhaps more by the mushroom cloud than by the Cross, so that we may find ourselves in a kind of despair or unacknowledged fatalism about the possibility of living by the Gospel vision, and of having that vision inform the social and political order. To prevent the coldness of indifference, or worse, of fatalism taking charge of our souls, we need to take the modest steps possible to us, and to take them consistently. I suggest that we need to take at least seven such steps.

First, we need *to remind* ourselves and all those we can reach, in season and out of season, of the Gospel teaching on nonviolence, of the nuclear threat, and of the implications of each. We may not allow ourselves the luxury of disengagement or indifference. This work of reminding must be nourished in attention, in prayer. We cannot possibly cope with the evil of the nuclear threat if we approach it only as a social or political problem. We are face to face with a mystery of iniquity which will be overcome only by a greater mystery of grace.

Second, we need *to interpret* the nuclear threat not only in terms of strategy and tactics, but also and especially in terms of good and evil. In this interpretation we can well be served by calling on the classic Catholic moral teaching on war, which has insisted on strict conditions, all of which must be present before participation in a war can be tolerated. These conditions cannot be met in using nuclear weaponry, and therefore we cannot acquiesce in a balance of terror based on a threat to use these weapons. In this work of interpretation we can link our disarmament work with human rights, developing an understanding of the right to refuse to kill. This right, like all human rights, is grounded in human dignity which is ours as the most beloved of God's creatures, made in his image, and redeemed not by gold and silver, but by the life, death, and resurrection of his son.

Third, we must *protest* not only the deployment but also the possession and manufacture of nuclear weapons. Strategies and tactics of protest may take many forms, but the act of protest in some nonviolent form is an integral part of a Christian peacemaking spirituality. In our situation, any spirituality would be suspect without some element of protest. As Christians we should base our protest on an affirmation of human dignity and freedom as we have come to know it through the revelation of God's love in Jesus, to whom we are united in a most intimate way. It is an affront to human dignity to engage in nuclear weapons manufacture or to ask others to spend their working lives in the manufacture of such weapons. We ought to bring the modern social teaching of the Church on the dignity of labor to bear on our nuclear weapons protest.

Fourth, we need *to advocate* alternatives to violence as a means of security. For some this will take the form of working for a particular disarmament initiative in the context of a nation's political framework; for others advocacy may mean laboring to bring into educational systems courses dealing with nonviolent conflict resolution, courses which can be based on an examination of actual cases which are too little known.

Fifth, we need *to build communities* of mutual support in our struggle. For this, we need to make serious investments of time and energy, commiting ourselves to endure through disappointments, errors, and failure. A Christian peacemaking spirituality is ultimately an act of faith. While faith is a personal act, it is not an individualistic one. A life of faith comes to us through a Christian community and is nurtured in community. Faced with the capacity to inflict unimaginable destruction on our single human family, we are being drawn to face the radical nature of the Christian Gospel in a way that may be for many of us a new and compelling experience. We cannot accept the Gospel, or hand it on, alone.

Sixth, we need *to care*. Milton Mayeroff, in his book, *On Caring*, says that we are at home in the world not by dominating, nor by understanding, nor even by appreciating, but by caring and being cared for. Perhaps the generation that comes after ours will be able to describe how badly our imaginations and emotions were damaged by the unleashing of atomic weaponry thirty-six years ago. To recover from nuclear numbness, or to protect itself from it, we need to exercise our ability to care in very specific ways. We need to care for each person as uniquely and infinitely precious in God's sight, and therefore in ours, if we are peacemakers deserving to be called children of God. This practice of caring will put us at the lovely risk of seeing each other as brothers and sisters, embarrassed by the artifacts that would deal only fratricide.

Finally, we need *to envision*, which is to say that we must allow ourselves to pay attention, to contemplate, to dream dreams and have visions, as did our ancestors who handed theirs down to us in song and poetry. We must never let go of those visions of the Holy Spirit, of a security founded on God's love. «The strength of the war horse means nothing to him, it is not infantry that interests him. Yahweh is interested only in those who fear him, in those who rely on his love.» (Psalm 147) We must keep our heart set on a kingdom in which «the wolf lives with the lamb, the panther lies down with the kid, in which the infant plays over the cobra's hole; and into the viper's lair the young child puts his hand. They do no hurt, no harm, ...for the country is filled with the knowledge of the Lord as the waters swell the sea.» (Isaiah 11: 6-9)

Prof. Joseph Comblin
THE CHURCH AND HUMAN RIGHTS

1. Human rights in the concrete

In Europe, afther the French revolution, as well as in the United States after independence, and even more in the former colonies that have recently obtained their independence, human rights very often mean, in the concrete, the rights of the middle class, the rights the middle class wants the State to grant. This often reminds us of the words of Lacordaire: freedom favours the rich and law defends the poor. Individual liberties and constitutional safeguards have often favoured the rich only and have even made the exploitation of the poor easier for them.

In the Christian sense of the word, human rights are the expression of two options of Jesus and, therefore, two options of God: the option in favour of the poor and the option in favour of sinners.

In the concrete, human rights must be the expression of the rights of the poor and promote their rights, confronting the privileges, the powers and the exploitation exerted by the rich and powerful. For we are face by an unequal society and so we must take sides.

In the concrete, human rights also become a problem when they are the rights of deviants or people who are considered, rightly or wrongly, to be dangerous. Those are the rights of deviants or sinners in the meaning of the Gospel. Today, in a world where the opposition between East and West is generally recognized as an absolute priority and a definitive criterion for any public action, national security has become one of the major obstacles of human rights. People are granted their rights provided they are conformists. But there is no right for 'communists' in the Western world, whether they are real or so-called communists, whereas in the communist world, there is no right for the real or so-called 'capitalists'. In such a context, the option in favour of sinners becomes particularly urgent.

Historically, there is often a confustion between the poor and sinners or deviants. The poor can indeed be considered, and they often are, as at least potential subversives. Because they are poor, they have reason not to be satisfied and they provide reserves for subversive forces.

2. Human rights and relations between developed and underdeveloped countries

Generally speaking, it is still true that the developed nations of the West support and maintain in power, in the Third World, the most corrupt elites and governments of the former colonial pact between the colonizing powers and the local elites. These are given major advantages and a share in Western wealth. In return, they maintain their populations in a state of order and submission. This is still true now. The Western powers help the governments who bend their people under the yoke. They grant the local elites extravagant privileges. So they are directly involved in all the violations of human rights. Besides, most of the time they intervene directly in order to teach the best methods of repression.

3. Who defends human rights?

The Church?

Within the Church, there are two competing lines, a diplomatic one and a spiritual one. According to the first, one must act in a diplomatic way in order to influence the authorities and save individuals. According to the other, one must give a testimony of truth and justice in order to save the credibility of faith and of the Church in the first place, even if one might, by doing so, diminish its power of intercession to save individuals.

The public authorities?

In many countries, public authorities are the main violators of human rights. One can of course call upon them, but there will be no result.

Solidarity among the workers?

In his last encyclical, Pope John Paul II primarily emphasizes solidarity among workers as a source of concrete historical change by which the workers manage to obtain new rights.

Supporting solidarity among the workers?

Development aid has usually been given in the form that was granted to the dominating states of developing countries. The question here is: what about aid from citizens of developed countries in favour of those who are being oppressed in the developing countries?

Jean-Marie Müller
PEACE SPIRITUALITY AND NONVIOLENCE

Spiritual and temporal

«*It is not God who makes war, but Man*». I would like to follow the line of this remark made by Cardinal Alfrink and conclude that therefore Man can make peace!

I have seen a poster saying «*Peace, gift of God. Prayer for Peace*». I am afraid this might lead to some kind of deadlock: in which meaning can we say that Peace is a gift of God? There are certainly many meanings in which we cannot say it, in which it would be a resignation to say it. I remember this prayer we used to say at the time I was a scout: «*Lord, bless this meal and give bread to those who do not have any*». Well, God is not going to give that bread if we do not do it ourselves. And it is not through this kind of intellectual swindling, of incredible pharisaism that we can ask God to do what *He* asks us to do: insofar as God does exist, *He* asks us to construct Peace.

I think that on that point, we have a permanent tendency to evade our responsibilities. God made us free and autonomous — thank God! We must therefore fundamentally distrust a disincarnate spirituality, because this is permanent temptation.

Father Friedli reminds us that when we are talking about the poor, these are not the feeble-minded and that when we are talking about the oppressed, this is indeed a political reality; consequently, the peace of God is not — as has too often been wrongly asserted — *solely* the peace of the soul and the heart and perhaps not even *in the first place* the peace of the soul and the heart.

And it seems to me that precisely christianity gives us a historical vision, and so it is in history that it is important to assert transcendency which can actually be the very foundation of christianity.

There has often been a false debate on what has been called 'horizontalism'. The 'theologians of liberation' have often been said to have fallen in the trap — some even say the heresy — of horizontalism. And this has also been one of the central themes when John Paul II was in Puebla. On the other hand, when considering the history of christianity, we see that the permanent temptation is one of a vertical spirituality, which, in my opinion, has not got anything to do with the Judeo-christian tradition. I very firmly believe that christianity has been polluted by platonism and that it has been suggested that pureness was to be sought outside the human conflict of history. I think that this is the heresy.

I would like to quote a few lines from Péguy which have strongly impressed me; Péguy insists on the unbreakable link between spiritual and temporal: «*We have to bear the expense of the temporal. Nobody can evade that, not even the Eternal, not even the Spiritual, not even the inner life. We have to bear the expense of the temporal, which means that nobody — not even the Church or any spiritual power — will come off without a temporal revolution. That is precisely the characteristic of christianity: this so extraordinary, so incredible encasing, adjusting of two pieces into each other and reciprocally of course, temporal into eternal, eternal into temporal. If they are released, there is nothing left, there is no more christianity, there are only debris with no name, materials with no shape, scraps and rubbish, confusion and disasters like those who we see, shameful forgeries, amorphous imitations, scandalous imaginations, foul parodies, odd heresies; there is no more christianity, no such point of overlapping left, no such marvellous unique «meeting» of the temporal in the Eternal and, reciprocally, of the Eternal in the temporal, of the divine in the human and, mutually, of the human in the divine*».

I think that in saying that, Péguy was revolting against which he called all the catechisms which have always tended to present a purified vision of christianity. So I believe that when we talk about spirituality of peace or spirituality in general, we should remember that it is only through the incarnation in the temporal, in history, in the present, that we can — I shall not simply say witness — but reach it.

I certainly do not want to ignore or despise the importance for each one of us, of a personal spiritual return to the sources, of having our roots in convictions that are beyond the economic, political, ideological problems. I do not want to reduce christianity to a historical and political vision, but I absolutely object to reducing christianity to an eschatological, prophetical, spiritual and, perhaps even worse than spiritual, a moral perspective.

And I believe that very often, we are indeed prisoners of moral categories, of a moralistic, idealistic position. And this is where we might very easily start side-slipping, by using big words which — of course — may have a profound and fundamental meaning but which might once again be nothing but empty shells, because they are actually no more surrounded by an environment likely to give them their entire living substance. These big words are ... universal Love, universal Reconciliation, Harmony, Justice, Freedom, Brotherhood... and they might be nothing but moral categories.

It seems to me that precisely when we talk about spirituality we should always start not from the ideal but from reality. And we will then soon realize that this reality stands in contrast with that ideal which we may and should carry within ourselves.

When, in the name of christian spirituality, we say «we are all brethren», what does that mean? Does that not already mean colliding with the temporal, historical, practical dimension of our existence in our relationship with the others, of whom we are obviously not the brethren, insofar as we do not have with them a brotherly relationship? So if we want to assert that beyond that conflictual reality there is a potentiality to build brotherly relationships, then my answer is yes. But instead of idealistically asserting that «we are all brethren», let us admit that we are not at all, and that it is not through any — even christian — magic formula or rite that we are going to succeed.

So we will have to spend some more time — as much time as will be required — on that conflictual reality, made of tensions, oppositions and, quite often, injustice, violence, sufferings, fear and death. I remember Father Régamay, a Dominican, who was one of the first to reflect on nonviolence. With regard to the songs we used to sing in our churches or in our temples, he said to me: «*if one reads through these texts beyond the singing, one is facing nothing but a delirium: how can we sing «Lord, the earth is ready to welcome you», while there is famine, oppression, destruction just everywhere... To say that we are ready to welcome Him is not only making fun of God; it is above all making fun of those who are being oppressed*».

We must therefore distrust spiritual, mystical delirium. If we spend some time on this reality made of oppositions, violence, fear, sufferings and death, the first thing we will have to do is not to resign ourselves to it and to reject any historical fatality. It is in that sense that the meaning of christianity is perhaps in the first place Hope, and a historical Hope, which I do not confine in History, but which should also have roots in History.

Legitimate violence?

From that point, this Hope must break the pagan fatality of violence. And also from this point of view, I am not sure that, finally, when asserting the eschatological spirituality of a world that will be made of brotherliness and reconciliation, we are not at the same time — and perhaps for that reason — resigned here and now to the situations of oppression, injustice and balance by terror. I am not sure that when we are so insistently reminded of the fact, that christian Hope can only be fully achieved in Eschatology, this is not one of the arguments used for finally resigning and accepting the fatality of the violence of our time better.

Is not the risk that, on the one hand, we might accept violence and take part in it ourselves in the name of a so-called realism and that, on the other hand, we profess an eschatological hope in a world of reconciliation, of happiness for everybody? So if we really want to ussume this reality of conflict, without avoiding it, without trying to seek whatever pureness outside history, we shall — without being ourselves caught in the wheels of violence — have to be able to find, invent, imagine, try a way to live through these conflicts, to solve them through another logic than the logic of violence. And I believe that we can only resort to a logic of nonviolence.

It is true that the word 'nonviolence' might be, at first, a little ambiguous. Father Schillebeeckx said that it was a negative word. Perhaps it would be better to take a closer look at things: in order to estimate the meaning of nonviolence, we must agree on the meaning of nonviolence. And if by violence we really mean a process of murder, of death, which really aims at killing someone else, or myself, well, I think we must then indeed refuse any process of justification, of legitimation of violence. Whether it is on the level of theology or philosophy, as long as we become aware of violence for what it is, i.e. the irruption of a process of murder in my relationship with the other, we can accept no argument which makes violence a right. As soon as violence becomes a right for man, I settle down in the practice of violence and I have no more feelings of contradiction, of contrast, which exists, through my existence, between reality and the ideal which is finally common to all spiritualities, to all religions.

And I believe that, indeed, in the history of christian theology, the function and the goal of the elaboration of the theology of «legitimate defense» was to justify violence. Besides, when nowadays we talk about the groups for «legitimate defence», we do justify violence and not defence. It is too obvious that defence is always legitimate when I am defending justice, my rights, and not my privileges.

So I believe that this theology of legitimate defence, of legitimate violence means a radical rupture with the evangelic dynamism. And I use the word dynamism, for I do not want to fall back into a form of legalism that would finally also become a dead letter. but, in order that this dynamism may really develop, I must indeed burst all the locks of the justification of violence, of war, of nuclear deterrence, etc.

For here again, christianity has become a morale, and christian morale has become a morale of intent. If you take a look at rather recent books on moral theology — and I am not sure that a lot of progress has been achieved in that field — regarding the problem of my relationship with the enemy, the fact of loving one's enemy, was to intend to love him, I would even say to love him in words, thoughts, omission, but not so much commission. So the fact of loving one's enemy did not mean not killing him, but it meant that we were to cleanse our intent so as to be ready to kill him with love. The sin would have been to kill him with hatred and I would have had to confess, not to having killed my enemy, but to the hatred I had felt when killing him. If I had killed him without hatred, then I was allowed to bear my decorations, even when receiving Holy Communion.

This is of course a piece of swindling, even from a philosophical point of view: I think that no philosophy can go as far as legitimating violence; I would even say that the philosophical awakening is precisely the fact of becoming aware of this contrast between violence and man's requirement of reconciliation. On the basis of that awareness, I can no longer justify violence.

And that is finally the meaning of nonviolence, which then becomes very positive: do you remember what they taught you at school: $(-) \times (-) = (+)$? Then, if we have a negative idea of violence, nonviolence becomes a prerequisite. It is only a prerequisite, but we have to be sure of that prerequisite: nonviolence, saying no to violence, refusing any ideological justification of violence; on the basis of that prerequisite, maybe we can start giving an answer. Bernanos said that in order to trust in the means that do not deceive, one must already despair of the means that do. So this is a prerequisite: but this prerequisite is so essential and, finally, so much rejected, that it seems to me that this nonviolent approach is absolutely decisive.

The role of conflict

Having said this, I would like to make a distinction — we know how important the vocabulary can be — between violence as such, which I defined as being a process of murder, and conflict, struggle, aggressiveness and strength. I think precisely that a spirituality of peace should not be a spirituality of reconciliation, but a spirituality of conflict, or, more exactly, that a spirituality of peace, that is a true spirituality of reconciliation, can only be a spirituality of conflict: if we start by rehabilitating conflict we can only really disparage violence.

Now, I believe that, generally speaking, spiritualities have always been worked out by disavowing conflict. That is why we talk about brotherhood, dialogue, confidence, love, justice, harmony: all of them are tremendously kind things, but finally, by being so kind, they become stupid and wicked. For, once again, the problem is to know how we can achieve reconciliation, how we can construct justice wherever there is injustice, how we can construct the peace that God will not give us unless we construct it ourselves, whereas there are wars everywhere.

On that level, we must clearly understand that conflict is not an evil, that it is essentially constructive: it is through conflict that I shall recognize the other and I must absolutely assume that moment of tension, adversity, opposition.

The christian requirement of loving the enemy is quite paradoxical. I think we should consider it as provocation. But for loving our enemies, there is a condition, and that is to have enemies. Perhaps we should insist more on the fact of having enemies than on the fact that we must then love them. And what will it mean then to love our enemies, if the relationship of enmity is recognized. Here again, let us withstand the temptation of idealism. Sometimes, nonviolence has been translated by using an expression from Gandhi «strength of truth», «strength of love». But just as in «*Peace, the gift of God*», there is a meaning in which this can be true, but there are many more meanings in which this is not true of course. For the very essence of love is to be powerless. And so there is not a strength of love that will constrain the privileged, the oppressor to recognize my rights.

We should not think either that christian spirituality compels us to achieve reconciliation only through the conversion of the other. For it may happen, of course, that people become converted (and that is certainly one of the reasons why we do not want to kill them) but, as Fricolli said, let us have a political and economic vision on things and, in the injust economic and political structures, we are not confronted with individuals, but with groups of interest, and a group of interests does not become converted, a multinational does not become converted.

Perhaps some leaders can become converted, but then they will leave and they will be replaced. So let us not dream and let us not say just anything in the name of our spirituality, inconsistent with the requirement of love and, I should even say of the possibility of love? A lot of rubbish has been told in this regard. Regarding the fact, for instance, that the Church ignored the class war, well we still have that now. I do not know if you have noticed: in all his texts, John Paul II always simultaneously condemns hatred and the class war. So we still find those old expressions, which the secretaries who prepare the encyclicals still have in their card-index. As if class war could only express itself through hatred and violence. So they ignored the class war and advocated love among classes. Cardinal Pius, in the XIXth century, advocated resignation of the poor, charity of the rich and happiness for everybody...

Those who talk about class war are still accused of being hideous marxists, communists, etc. Of course there is a war between classes that have contradictory interests; of course the conflict cannot be solved only through fraternal dialogue. It is the other way round: dialogue does not solve the conflict, it is the conflict that will solve the dialogue: the role of the conflict will be to make dialogue possible. For dialogue is impossible in a situation of injustice and oppression: dialogue requires equality between both partners. And hence an equality of power, not only an equality of theoretical dignity of being sons of the same Father, but a historical, temporal equality of rights and hence of **powers.**

Primacy of action

With respect to that, it seems to me that what is finally important, in the very coherence of this spirituality, is action. I do not believe in a spirituality that is not embodied in action.

We must be extremely careful when talking about spirituality, about ours of course, but especially about that of others. It is God who sounds the kidneys and the hearts, so on which basis can we judge whether someone is spiritual or not? I admire those who have a discernment enabling them to do so, but, thank God, I do not have that charism in any case!

What precisely appears to me as a criterion is not what is in the inner life (and which is, of course, invisible), but in the external life. Besides, I regret that the expression 'inner life' has been chosen to express 'spiritual life'. Love always expresses itself towards the outside.

Therefore, it seems to me that the criterion of spirituality is precisely action for justice, action for peace, action for reconciliation. That is why I am interested in 'orthopractice', not in 'orthodoxy'. It is not the rigour of the discourses, of the dogma, of the rite we are quarrelling about. Rome has made more fuss over Father Schillebeeckx than over all the bishops who justify nuclear armament, as if for the very meaning of christianity, stretching a little the dogma as described in books was more harmful than finally denying the dynamism of hope and of love as embodied by Christ in Galilee, nearly 2,000 years ago.

Therefore: orthopractice. Besides, we can read in the Gospel that the criteria for salvation are criteria at the level of action: «I was hungry ...» — this year, 30 to 40 million people will die of starvation... it is not only the poor who beg in front of the church!

«*I was in prison...*» we are not only talking about the thief or the murderer but about all the political prisoners and we know what that means nowadays. The alien, the entire problem of immigration,...

So that is finally the definitive criterion for what is called «Judgement Day». Constructing that justice without falling back ourselves in the wheels of violence, finally becomes very quickly a problem of efficient technique, strategy. We know, of course, that techniques are not neutral and we have precisely to take violence as a technique. Personally, I do not judge those who use violence, I do not even question their spirituality, nor their peace spirituality, for that would mean that I judge them.

Sometimes I give lectures in Trappist monasteries and I tell them: «*You have chosen a life made entirely of contemplation, you have refused every action in the world because, compared with your meditation, it was a «diversion», in the meaning Pascal would have given to that word. There is, however, an action which you do not refuse: and that is war. When your respective States mobilize you, you leave your frocks in the sacristy and you run to the barracks to dress in Caesar's uniform!*» Now, if there is one action that should have diverted them from their contemplation, it is precisely that one. And still I cannot accuse them of not having a spiritual life, of not taking their time to pray and meditate on the Scriptures.

The importance of the technique

So, it is not a problem of spirituality but of technique. There is something wrong with the technique, with the means. Nonviolence does not pretend to be a new spirituality. What is brilliant about Gandhi is the fact that he was able to implement a strategy that enabled the Indians to free themselves from British colonialism without falling back into the wheels of violence. If Gandhi had not come, nor anyone else, there would inevitably have been a liberation by violence and people would have said, as one could also say in different situations: «As you can see, only violence could liberate India».

What seems essential to me, is to invest in the knowledge of those techniques of nonviolent action. I think that also in the debate about the problem of defence, we cannot just assert — but it is already a big achievement if we do — that, as far as nuclear disarmament is concerned, unilateral disarmament in our country certainly is the position that is closest to the Gospel. It is very important to say it, but we should also be aware that this does not mean that we shall not have to face conflicts, aggression. And I would even say that in front of public opinion, it will not be that easy to convince that public opinion that this unilateral disarmament step is essential, if we cannot at the same time convince it that there are other ways to defend ourselves, other techniques to resist, to deal with an invasion of Soviet paratroopers, or others...

So we are indeed required to propose an alternative to violence as a technique of action. Otherwise, we will keep wavering between violence and love.

As an example, I shall quote a speech John Paul II made during his visit in Ireland, where he very clearly condemned violence (here again, the violence of the citizens, unfortunately; he does 'regret' the violence of the State, but his condemnation is much less categorical. It is a pity he does not see it the other way round.) «*Violence is an evil; it is unacceptable, it is not worthy of man, it is a lie, because it goes against the truth of our faith, the truth of our humanity. It destroys what it pretends to defend, the freedom of human beings. Violence is a crime against humanity, for it destroys the very texture of society*». And so on.

Perfect! I agree. But what comes after? The apology of love, of forgiveness, of reconciliation.. .but how can the Irish, involved in all these conflicts, starting from violence, come to this idyllic vision? The essential is lacking and that is precisely to try and propose, suggest nonviolent methods of action, capable of living through the conflict, of making the conflict evolve, towards justice. In other words, I could summarize by saying that reconciliation is only possible in justice and that justice is only possible through a struggle, and that, finally, a true struggle is only possible through nonviolent action. I think that if we forget one of those three assertions, we are not working at the level of reality.

Then we have also got to define what this praxis of non-violence means. But first of all, I would like to challenge somewhat the perspective that was proposed by someone who said non-violence is the 'square of utopia'. I believe it is exactly the opposite, I mean non-violence seen through the experience of Gandhi, King, Chavez, Walesa today. What looks like the square of utopia to me is forgiveness, reconciliation, etc. But non-violence, seen through the experience of Gandhi and insofar as it is a technique of action aiming at efficiency — and perhaps with better chances than violence — well, that non-violent action, in reality, wants to depart at the same time from the false realism of violence and the devilish idealism of love.

Prof. Gerard A. Vanderhaar
THE NEW VISION ON PEACE AND
NONVIOLENCE

A new vision of the human family is necessary in order to work effectively for peace in the face of the challenges of the Nuclear Age. The nuclear threat hanging over our planet reveals the inadequacy of the old vision of people grouped together in nations, prepared to assert their rights and defend their way of life by violence.

The Old Vision

The dominant theme of national security has been, as expressed in the Roman proverb, *si vis pacem, para bellum*, if you want peace, prepare for war. The assumption was that peace comes through strength: aggressors are deterred by the power and might of their would-be victims.

The illusion that violence is a way to peace has been shattered by two 20th century events: Auschwitz and Hiroshima. Ten million people died in the Nazi concentration camps. Many of these millions were victims of the ideology of racial purity. Others were victims of religious prejudice. All were killed because they were considered in some way dangerous to national security.

If it is permissible to kill one person for a cause considered legitimate, then it is permissible to kill a million and more if necessary, and possible. Technological sophistication and organizational techniques developed during World War II made mass murder on an unprecedented scale possible. The death camps, a direct result of the willingness to use violence in pursuit of one's goals, shocked the world. So did the bombing of Hiroshima. 100,000 men, women and children died in the fiery flash of the first atomic bomb. Thousands more carried death in their bodies for weeks and months, until they collapsed from radiation poisoning.

Prompt pursuit of the power of the atom resulted in the thermonuclear weapons of our time, which threaten the extinction of hundreds of millions of people in every part of the world in a blaze that would make the Nazi holocaust seem a bonfire by comparison.

Auschwitz and Hiroshima have emerged as symbols, in the words of one historian, «of the capacity of the modern state to justify mass murder, and of the inability of most civilians, especially in time of war, to affirm the humanity of the enemy or to oppose the brutal practices of their own state.»

A Time of Grace

Now, in the mysterious providence of God, we have a time of grace. We have time to face the atrocities of the past, probe their implications, and use our accumulated wisdom to prevent much greater atrocities in the future. We recognize certain constants in human nature. One of them is the power to hurt and kill other human beings. Another is our ability to perceive social pressures, and to rise above them. Two such pressures that fuel the threat hanging over all of us today are national loyalty, and the logic of violence.

Truth Before Loyalty

Albert Camus once wrote, «All I ask is that, in the midst of a murderous world, we agree to reflect on murder and to make a choice. After that, we can distinguish those who accept the consequences of being murderers themselves or the accomplices of murderers, and those who refuse to do so with all their force and being.»

Camus' insight shines as a beacon light in the complex and morally murky world of the late 20th century. Pilate's age-old question, what is truth, is particularly difficult to answer in the complicated and confused arena of international maneuverings. But if we can identify murder and preparations for murder in death camps, torture of dissidents, and nuclear weapons, then we can choose which side of those activities we want to be on.

Father Daniel Berrigan, the American Jesuit priest and peace activist, proclaimed this truth at his trial earlier this year for destroying nose cones of nuclear missiles at a General Electric plant. «It's terrible for me to live in a time where I have nothing to say to human beings except, «Stop killing.» There are other beautiful things that I would love to be saying to people. There are other projects I could be very helpful at. And I can't do them. I can't.

«Because everything is endangered. Everything is up for grabs. Ours is a kind of primitive situation, even though we would call ourselves sophisticated. Our plight is very primitive from a Christian point of view. We are back where we started. Thou shalt not kill; we are not allowed to kill. Everything today comes down to that--everything.»

The choice to become - or resist becoming - accomplices to the mass murder contemplated by modern governments provides us with a rare moment of truth. If our decision takes us beyond national loyalties, so much the worse for national loyalties. The truth, at least this once, becomes clear.

Jesus said, «All who take the sword will perish by the sword» (Matt. 26:52). By agreeing with the deployment and threatened use of nuclear weapons we are taking up the most destructive sword yet forged by human skill. It is likely that in the remaining years of our century we will all perish by this sword.

But before we perish physically we are already perishing spiritually. Living with the intention to commit mass murder is psychologically disturbing and morally corrosive. A nation with this burden on its conscience can expect a severe deterioration in its internal morality. Its citizens will much more easily rationalize lesser crimes. The nuclear weapons may destroy our bodies, wrote American theologian Richard McSorley, «but our intent to use nuclear weapons destroys our souls.»

Loyalty to community, company or country should never obscure the imperative of facing these facts. Loyalty can cover a multitude of sins. Truth demands that loyalty be put in second place when the good of people is at stake. And so we choose truth and life, before loyalty - and death.

The Human Family

Teilhard de Chardin wrote, «The age of nations is past. The task before us now, if we would not perish, is to shake off our ancient prejudices, and to build the earth.»

Jesus taught that the supreme guide to life was love of neighbor. Neighbor is anyone in need, regardless of religious or national differences. Paul wrote that «there is neither Jew nor Greek, there is neither slave nor free, there is neither male nor female, for you are all one in Christ Jesus» (Gal. 3:28). Paul saw the essential unity of everything in Christ Jesus, a unity which transcended racial, class and sex differences.

This broad concern for the human family has characterized the lives of more and more people in the last two decades of this century. As Gerald and Patricia Mische have written, «There is today a growing consciousness of the fact that we are unalterably bound together. We share a common dependency on one earth system. We stand together in relationship with one air, water, land, and life-support system. We have the same needs, the same potentialities, the same capacities for participating in destruction or for participating in creation.»

The mandate we have from Jesus is to «go into all the world and preach the gospel to the whole creation» (Mark 16:15). The gospel, the good news, is that we are redeemed, we are no longer victims of our sinful nature, but rather citizens of the Kingdom of God - all of us.

The Logic of Violence

Our desire for peace in the face of the nuclear threat, which impels us beyond national loyalties, also helps us reject the logic of violence. This logic, which leads inexorably from small weapons for personal defense, to internal security forces, to military services employing sophisticated weapons, points right up to thermonuclear warheads aimed at cities.

Once the logic of violence is rejected because of its nuclear implications, the legitimacy of any killing of human beings is removed.

Throughout history there have been some few who have been so impressed by the horrors of war that they have refused to take part in it. Their convictions, stemming from humanitarian inclinations or biblical faith, form the basis of classical pacifism. To their number have now been added scores of new pacifists, who came to nonviolence by a different route.

Daniel Berrigan has said that in the context of nuclear weapons «no principle is worth the sacrifice of a single life.» The reason is that in the interconnected, troubled world in which we live, it is conceivable that an initial act of violence could lead, in perhaps no more than a half-dozen escalations, to ultimate, almost infinite violence. Because of this awesome possibility, the absolute injunction embodied in the commandment «Thou shalt not kill» takes on a new wisdom in the Nuclear Age.

But the wisdom is at odds with the conventional «wisdom» of our societies. Fortunately, providentially, in the same century in which God has allowed us to see the terrible depths to which human beings can sink, He also raised up for us prophets of a new way - people like Gandhi, Martin Luther King and, yes, Daniel Berrigan. They have taught us not only what true peace means, but have been living examples of the way to reach it.

Positive Peace

Peace is not just the absence of the quick killing through physical violence. It is also the absence of the slow killing through structural violence. Peace is a positive condition in which people are free, not exploited, living so they can grow to their full potential. Peace involves, as theologian Joseph Fahey has described it, not only a low level of physical and psychological violence, but also a high level of economic and social justice. The vision of positive peace exerts a powerful pull. It puts the focus on meeting the needs of people wherever they are, by whatever forces they are threatened. This is the humanitarian call. It is also the Christian call capsuled in the commandment to love one's neighbor as oneself, which, as Saint Paul remarked, sums up all the other commandments (Rom. 13:9).

End and Means

Many in our world today believe that violence is at times a legitimate way of fulfilling this commandment of love. But Gandhi has reminded us that the means are inseparable from the end. As A.J. Muste, founder of the Fellowship of Reconciliation, put it: «There is no way to peace, peace is the way.»

Gandhi used an image from nature: «The means may be likened to a seed, the end to a tree.» The means by which peace is obtained must be peaceful themselves. Otherwise it is a false peace, a sham, a mask for repression and violence.

Martin Luther King's insight that our choice today is not between violence and nonviolence, but between nonviolence and non-existence, is another of those beacons of truth that illuminate the darkness of our age. Truth calls for us to stand nonviolently, to walk nonviolently, and to work nonviolently for peace in justice.

The American President Abraham Lincoln once said, «I destroy my enemies when I make them my friends.» Lincoln's words and the difficult course of action they imply deserve our careful attention in these difficult times. With personal enemies we seek forgiveness and reconciliation. With national enemies we urge communication and negotiation.

The Nonviolent Cross

The nonviolent path to peace is not easy. Those who take it will be misunderstood by some, denounced by others, and probably persecuted by agents of the principalities and powers of this world.

Gandhi once said, «Just as one must learn the art of killing in the training for violence, so one must learn the art of dying in the training for nonviolence.»

Martin Luther King preached, «To our most bitter opponents we say: We shall match your capacity to inflict suffering by our capacity to endure suffering. We shall meet your physical force with our soul force.»

As Bishop Carroll Dozier of Memphis has written, «In the struggle for peace, the shadow of the cross falls across our own lives. We take up the burdens of peacemaking, remembering that Jesus said, 'Come to me, all who labor and are heavy laden, and I will give you rest. Take my yoke upon you and learn from me; for I am gentle and lowly in heart, and you will find rest for your souls. For my yoke is easy, and my burden is light' (Matt. 11:28-30).»

Conclusion

The courageous witness of those people like Gandhi and King and Berrigan who have stood for truth and love in the face of injustice and violence gives encouragement to all who are pursuing the path of peace today.

The vision of reality to guide us through the Nuclear Age includes all of the human race, in splendid diversity, forming a single human family, beyond the artificial boundaries of culture, creed and nation. Conflicts will exist, as they do in all families. But efforts to resolve them will be nonviolent.

Fulfilling that vision calls for a new determination, a new will to take concerted action to translate the vision from dream to reality.

Dom Benoit Standaert o.s.b.
PRAYER AND PEACE

Numbers 6, 22-27

*22. The Lord said to Moses, 23. «Say
to Aaron and his sons, Thus you shall
bless the people of Israel: you shall say
to them,
24. The Lord bless you and keep you:
25. The Lord make his face to shine upon
you, and be gracious to you:
26. The Lord lift up his countenance upon
you, and give you peace.
27. «So shall they put my name upon
the people of Israel, and I will bless them».*

Psalms 122, 6-9

*6. Pray for the peace of Jerusalem!
«May they prosper who love you!
7. Peace be within your walls,
and security within your towers!»
8. For my brethren and companions
sake
I will say, «Peace be within you!»
9. For the sake of the house of the
Lord of God,
I will seek your good.*

1 Timothy 2, 1-4, 8

2. First of all, then, I urge that suppli-
cations, prayers, intercessions and thanks
givings be made for all men, for kings
and all who are in high positions,
that we may lead a quiet and peaceable
life, godly and respectful in every way.
This is good, and it is acceptable in the
sight of God our Saviour, who desires
all men to be saved and to come to the
knowledge of the truth (...)
8. I desire then that in every place the
men should pray, lifting holy hands
without anger or quarrelling;

Matthew 5, 44-45

44. But I say to you, Love your enemies and
pray for those who persecute you, 45. so that
you may be sons of your Father who is in
heaven; for he makes his sun rise on the evil
and on the good, and sends rain on the just
and on the unjust.

Three keytexts of the biblical tradition will be the starting point of our common reflexion on the relation between prayer and peace and vice versa. We will also refer to the Jewish tradition of which the liturgical tradition and the comments are a unique witness to understand better the biblical text cited herewith. The monastic way of living, which is mine, will also offer some reflexion on this theme. Other ways of living will explain in their way the link between peace and prayer. Finally we may expect an enrichment resulting from the different approaches and from the exchange of views following this introduction.

1. A first text (Nb. 6, 23-27) explains at the same time the nature of peace and the sense of prayer with regard to peace.

*«Say to Aaron and his sons, Thus you shall
bless the people of Israel: you shall say
to them,
The Lord bless you and keep you:
The Lord make his face to shine upon
you, and give you peace.
So shall they put my name upon the people of
Israel and I will bless them.»*

It concerns a benediction (berakha). It is essential to the life of prayer of the Jewish community, up to the present (1). In the berakha, man blesses God and God on his part promises to bless humankind. Prayer is called: «to put the name of God upon the people ofIsrael». It is an act of mankind but it appeals to an act of God. It concerns the Name of God, the radiance of his Face, the gift of peace. Peace, as final point, is linked up with the Name of God, his uncovered Face, his clear proximity. It is difficult to give it a precise content. Peace seems to cover an including reality which meets the wishes of those who are blessed but which also surpasses anything one can imagine since it is in the first place a gift of the Lord who uncovers his Face. Peace implies a highly personal relationship between the Lord and his people. In this sense one can say: there will be no peace without the Alliance between God and his people.

In the same line one can remember the words of the Psalmist:

*«Let me hear what God the Lord will speak,
for he will speak peace to his people,
to his saints, to those who turn
to him in their hearts».*

(Ps. 85, 8, and following)

2. A second series of texts treat prayer in connection with peace, as an intercession. We refer to two witnesses:

«Pray for the peace of Jerusalem!
May they prosper who love you!
Peace be within your walls,
and security within your towers!»
For my brethren and companions' sake
I will say, «Peace be within you!»
For the sake of the house of the
Lord our God,
I will seek your good.
(Ps. 122, 6-9)

First of all then, I urge that supplications, prayers, inter-
cessions and thanksgivings be made for all men, for kings and all
who are in high positions, that we may lead a quiet and peaceable
life, godly and respectful in every way. This is good and it is ac-
ceptable in the sight of God our Saviour, who desires all men to
be saved and to come to the knowledge of the truth (...). I desire
then that in every place the men should pray, lifting holy hands
without anger or quarrelling;» (1 Tim. 2, 1-4.8)

These are two classical texts. The first supposes that one remembers the etymology of the name Jerusalem, city of peace (salem shalom) (1a). The second, the intercession, is especially recommended to the men («andres», v. 8). It concerns moreover all human beings, since it is rooted in the universal love of God himself (who desires all men to be saved» v. 4). This love showed itself in the one mediator, «the man Christ Jesus» (v. 55). intercession will thus be called «universal prayer». More particularly is it connected with the intercession of the one mediator between God and humankind, Christ Jesus (see also Ro., 34; He 7, 25; 1 Jn 2, 1-2 where Christ, raised from the dead, intercedes continually for us).

Intercession is recommended «everywhere» which adds to its universality. In addition the apostle desires «holy hands without anger or quarelling». In the prayer for peace there is a demand for life. «No prayer in a heart filled with resentment» says l'Abbé du Sinaï Jean Climaque (VII Century). And the Jewish tradition adds to it: «The wise said: Anyone who seeks peace, can be sure that his prayer will not come back to him without being heard» (2). In the midrash one can read: «There can be no efficient benediction if it is not associated to peace, because the seal of every prayer is peace, just as the sacerdotal benediction is sealed with peace». (Bamidbar Rabba 11, 16).

In the book of Job the prayer of an innocent man turns into a person that vouches for him:

«*Although there is no violence in my hands,*
and my prayer is pure.
Even now, behold, my witness is in heaven
and he that vouches for me is on high.
My friends scorn me;
my eye pours out tears to God,
that he would maintain the right of
a man with God,
like that of a man with his neighbour»
(Job 16, 17.19-22)

In the further exhortation of the apostle one can find many intercessions for peace in the different liturgies. Remember the many intercession litanies during the Holy Liturgy of the Christians of Byzantine rite. In the first two prayers following the Lord's Prayer of the Latins we state the following words: Libera nos quaesumus ... da pacem in diebus nostris ... et Domine Jesu Christi qui dixisti (...) Pacem relinquo vobis, pacem meam do vobis ...

It is interesting to remember that the kiss of peace following these two intercessions, originally came after the intercession and before the presentation of the gifts (cfr. Justin, Apol. I, 65). It was used as conclusion for the prayer: *osculum pacis quod est signaculum orationis* (Tertullien, *de orat.* 18: see also *Traditio apostolica* 21 (Botte 55); Origène, *In Rom hom* 10, 33 (PG 14, 12 82s.) who comments Rom 16, 16 and points out: *mos ecclesiiis traditus est up post orationes osculo invicem suscipiant fratres.* According to Saint Benedict the host only receives the kiss of peace after a common prayer, *Regula* c. 53. Several comments interpret the place of the rite of the kiss of peace, before the offertory, in the ligth of Mt. 5, 23 ss.: «So if you are offering your gift at the altar, and there remember that your brother has something against you, ...(3)

We also mention the prayer *Hanc igitur* of the Latins, introduced by Pope Gregory the Great in the ancient roman canon. This prayer took the place of the different possible formules to introduce the intention of the Mass. Saint Gregory simply unified the prayer by generalizing it: *diesque nostros in tua pace disponas atque ab aeterna damnatione nos eripi et in electorum tuorum jubeas grege numerari.*

The demand: «arrange our days in your peace» could be an allusion to the menaces of invasion by the Goths (4). The most powerful formulation of the Latins is without any doubt the one in the third eucharistic prayer of the rite after Vatican Council II. The idea is expressed in each of the three new prayers. Let's take the prayer that seems to us the most significant: «*And now we beg you Lord, through the sacrifice that unites us, spread peace and salvation over the whole world.*»

The idea that Christ's sacrifice reconciles and that the dimensions of salvation and peace are destined to include the whole world and even the whole creation, prepare directly our third point (5).

3. A third series of texts reveals the real limits of prayer for peace. Let's take as starting point the recommendation of Jesus at the end of the first part of the Sermon of the Mount:

> «*But I say to you, Love*
> *your enemies and pray for those*
> *who persecute you so that you*
> *may be sons of your Father who is*
> *in heaven, for he makes his sun rise*
> *on the evil and on the good, and sends*
> *rain on the just and on the unjust*»
> (Mt. 5, 44-45)

Prayer here is compared with the love of enemies. One strengthens the other one. Saint Benedict has the following precept in his rule (VIth century): In Christi amore pro inimicis orare». This expression refers not only to the passage cited above of the Sermon on the Mount, but also Christ's death on the Cross and his prayer for his enemies: *Father, forgive them; for they know not what they do*». (Lk. 23, 34) cfr. The prayer of Stephen who was stoned: «*Lord, do not hold this sin against them*». (Ac 7, 60).

That this prayer is associated with the love of God can undoubtly be explained by the reminiscence of the Pauline writings and especially of ch. 5 of the letter of Paul to the Romans: «... *But God shows his love for us in that while we were yet sinners Christ died for us.* (v. 8). *For, if while we were enemies we were reconciled to God by the death of his Son...* (v. 10, cfr. Ro 8, 31 ss; 2 Cor 5, 14-21; etc.). The love for enemies as well as the prayers for our persecutors never come of themselves and all the texts that treat this subject reveal a long process of suffering and patience, lived before God. It concerns a mystery, a hereafter of everything dependent on our natural resources.

It is a question of proposing untiringly and of living already the reciprocity with those who refuse every kind of relation. That is akin to the paradox, the «stumbling block» and the «scandals» as Saint Paul said (1 Cor. 1, 23).

The Evangelic Gospel and the liturgy contain plenty of these paradoxes especially when peace is introduced. Two witnesses can help us in realizing better this limit. A recent interview with Dalaï Lama, published by Fr. Jean Yves Leloup in «Vie spirituelle» 134 (1980) pp. 634-638 contains this final paragraph (638): *The compassion the Mahayana Buddhism talks about is not the ordinary love that we feel for those who are close and dear to us: this love can coexist with egoism and ignorance. We must also love our enemies. If I do all I can to help a person and if this person outrages me in the most disgraceful way, could I consider this person as my greatest master?*

If our friends are on good terms with us and are close to us, there is nothing that can make us aware of our negative thoughts. It is only when we are attacked and criticized that we can get to know ourselves and that we can judge the quality of our love. Our enemies are also our greatest masters. They allow us to test our strength, our tolerance, our respect for others. If we love our enemies even more, instead of hating them, we are close to reaching the state of Buddha, the eliminated conscience which is the aim of all the religions.

Even in the Starets Silouane (Mount Athos + 1938) there are entire pages on this «love of enemies» associated to prayer and peace. He himself refers to Séraphim de Sarov and his master Jean de Cronstadt about whom he writes: *thus praying constantly for the people (Lord, I wish that your peace may rest on your people...»), he kept his soul in peace; but we, we lose peace because we do not love our enemies. The holy apostles and the saints wish that there would be salvation in the whole world and staying among the people, they prayed ardently for them. The Holy Spirit gave them the strength to love men. As far as we are concerned, if we do not love our brother, we cannot live in peace». He who has not received the Holy Spirit does not want to pray for his enemies. Abba Païssios prayed for one of his disciples who had rejected Christ and while he was praying the Lord appeared and said: «Païssios for whom are you praying? Don't you know that he denied me?» But the Saint still had compassion on his disciple and the Lord said to him «Païssios, through your love you assimilate yourself to me». That's how we find peace, and there's no other way. He who has the peace of the Holy Spirit within him spreads this peace on the others: but he who bears the spirit of evil in him, spreads evil on others. It is a great work for God to pray for those who offend us and who make us suffer. In turn the Lord will give you his grace, you will know the Lord through the Holy Spirit and you will endure all the sorrows with joy because of him. The Lord will tell you to love the whole world. You will wish ardently good for all men and for yourself. The Lord has told us: Love your enemies and he who loves his enemies resembles the Lord. But one can only love his enemies through the grace of the Holy Spirit.* (cfr. Archimandrite Sophrony, Starets Silouane, éd. Présence 1973, pp. 292 and 294)

There are many paradoxes in the Gospel and Liturgy when peace is introduced. We mention 3 passages: In Saint John, on the first day of the week, the risen Christ appeared to the disciples: «*the doors being shut for fear of the Jews. He said to them: «Peace be with you». When he had said this, he showed them his hands and his side*». (Jn. 20, 19-20). The word «peace» is as it were verified in the signs of the passion he undeniably suffered. «*I have said this to you that in me you may have peace. In the world you may have tribulation; but be of good cheer, I have overcome the world*» (Jn 16, 33). Peace appears as the fruit of Christ's passion and death, within the Church that suffered persecution.

A second example, almost too well known to strike our senses, is when Christ broke the bread (cfr. Lk 24, 30-31). In the liturgy this gesture is immediately associated with the gift of peace (see the song of the Agnus Dei, that coincides with the breaking of the bread and the request: *Give us peace*). The breaking of the bread reminds us immediately of the distribution of the bread at the Last Supper and means the voluntary death of the Saviour. By accepting this piece of bread the faithful are united in God's gesture, take part in his Spirit and accept forgiveness and peace.

He who was thus broken and crushed by mankind, who was nailed to the Cross is also the one who breaks and destroys every kind of resistance, hostility and creates this gesture of death a new being, reconciliation for everybody. This victorious dimension of the death on the Cross has nowhere been confirmed so strongly in the NT as in Ephés 2.

«For he (Christ Jesus) is our peace,
who has made us both one,
and he has broken down the dividing wall
of hostility, by abolishing in his flesh the
law of commandments and ordinances,
that he might create in himself one
new man in place of the two, so making peace,
and might reconcile us both to God in one
body through the cross, thereby bringing
the hostility to an end. And he came and
preached peace to you who were far off and
peace to those who were near;
for through him we both have access in
one Spirit to the Father» (2, 14-18)

This text refers constantly to the moment when Christ was crucified. But all the verbs that express what Jesus went through, are this time used in the active tense: It is he, broken down, who broke down the dividing wall, he who, was killed, *«abolished the law of commandments and ordinances»*, he who united, reconciled, gave peace and opened the way to God the Father; while he was rejected, condemned and who had to undergo the malediction of the Law: *«Cursed be everyone who hangs on a tree»* (Dt. 21, 23; Gal 3, 13). In the middle of the kenosis or the annihilation of Christ on the Cross, in this *«love to the very end»* Saint John speaks of, a new order is set up, a new peace that the world cannot give.

Divine act par excellence, reconciliation and communion between all men and God. (6) This order is only perceived and can only be communicated, by those who - in whichever way - even outside the christian confession, are united in his only Son in his surrender and who are attracted by the radiance of the face of the Risen Christ.

CONCLUSION

The prayer for peace is berakha: benediction and recognizance of God by mankind, benediction and gift of God to those who live in his alliance. The prayer for peace is universal intercession. In the freedom that characterizes the life between God and humankind, prayer intervenes so that he would use his freedom for those he wants to save in Jesus Christ. Such a prayer needs a pure heart «lifting holy hands without anger or quarrelling (1 Tim 2, 8).

The prayer for other people, even when they cannot or when they do not want a relation with us, is an excellent christian school. Prayer and peace are united in some men who radiate it in spite of themselves in the middle of the worst trials, conflict and even violence. He who strives for peace will be a man of prayer because prayer is a gift of God in the Alliance, and the real man of prayer only wants at the bottom of his heart peace for all men for the whole universe that was created. Peace is a way that will lead us for certain if we commit ourselves with our entire being close to the place where the divine benevolence lies. This place was known and recognized by the patriarchs, prophets and Judges (Abraham, Gen. 22, Moses (ex 3) Gideon (Jug 6) etc.) Place of the perfect sacrifice, place of the fire, of the pure obligations, place of the new eternal alliance, christian place par excellence. The point is to join and to be connected with the point where the crucified and risen Christ intercedes constantly for us and reconciles the Universe with the Creator. Each moment may be a step in this direction

> «when the day shall dawn upon us
> from on high to guide our feet into
> the way of peace (Lc 1, 78-79). Amen»

(1) The history of the role of the sacerdotal benediction in the Jewish liturgy was described very well by I. Elbogen, Der Jüdische Gottesdienst in seiner geschitlichen Entwicklung, Hildesheim 1967 (= Frankfurt 3, 1931), pp. 67-72. See also E. Munk, The World of Prayer, vol. I, New York 1961, pp. 49-50; 155-158, and A.Z. Idelsohn, Jewish Liturgy and Its Development, New York 3, 1975, pp. 107-108.

(1a) As city of «peace» Jerusalem becomes a universal city. According to the Jewish vision (cfr. already Is 2, 1-5; 45, 14; 56, 1—8, etc.) the particular and the universal are not contradictory or do not exclude each other, but they are united and depend on each other. With regard to prayer we state here what Rabbi Israël Baal Shem Tov, the founder of the hassidism wrote among many others: «When a Jew hopes and prays for the dedemption of Israël he has to take into account that the whole world waits for redemption because the whole creation is in exile, subject to the forces of evil owing to the fact the celestial vases were broken and a man has to devote his efforts to eternal salvation, to the salvation of all the world together with Israël.» See anthological essay of Arie Eliav, Shalom, Peace in Jewish Tradition, Massadah 1977.

(2) Derek Eretz Zuta, in the chapter consecrated to peace.

(3) See J.A. Jungmann, Missarum solemnia, II, Herder 5, 1962, pp. 399-413

(4) See J.A. Jungmann, op. cit., II, pp. 231-232.

(5) In the Jewish tradition the great prayer of the 18 benedictions ends with the prayer of peace just as at the end of the service the sacerdotal benediction is introduced of the Nb 6, 24-26, followed by two prayers for peace: Sim Shalom et Shalom Rav. A.Z. Idelsohn (op. cit., p. 108) states that a prayer similar to Sim Shalom is mentioned in the Talmud (b. Ber. 55 b: addir bammarom: «Glorious on high, abiding in might, Thou art peace and Thy Name is peace; may it be Thy will to grant us peace». The Midrash writes: «Great is peace, because all the benediction and words of comfort that the Saint, may He be blessed, brings to Israël end with the invocation of peace:
- after the recitation of Listen Israël: «You who spread the tabernacle of peace»
- in the Amidah prayer: «You who make peace»
- in the sacerdotal benediction «May he give you peace» (Vayikra Rabba, 9, 9).

110

(6) The Jewish tradition insists on the practice that the prayer for peace can only take place once the sacrifice is accomplished (Lev. 9, 22). The Jewish tradition cites examples of Noah, the first who offered a sacrifice to God which resulted in a benediction for all men, Gen. 8, 9; and the example of Abraham, Gen. 22, when Abraham tied up his son Isaac followed by a benediction on all his descendants. Besides the exegesis of the great sacerdotal benediction connects three main types of sacrifice (hata's, 'olah, shelamin) with each of the three benedictions which constitute the prayer of the Nb 6, 24-26. See E. Munk, op. cit. pp. 49-50. Elsewhere: «The birkat khohanim forms the closing link in the chain of the 18 blessings. It is not an isolated, independent act. Only as a result of the preceding 'avodah, the service, can the blessings pronounced in it, and culminating in the blessing of peace, be obtained. Peace is, as the Rabbis express it, «the vessel containing and preserving all blessings». It is no the first preceding avodah and hodah; for our peace is perfect only if it grows out of common gratitude and common submission to the service of His Law» (op. cit., p. 156).

Dom C.J.A. Tholens o.s.b.
MEDITATION, CONTEMPLATION, REFLECTION

I. A few words of Pope John XXIII in his Document 'Pacem in Terris' may be the starting point for the discussion in our Workgroup 'Peace and Prayer'. Pope John stresses that «*we have to be in this world luminous sparks, centres of love and a leaven for peace through our union with God*» (Pacem in Terris, 164). «*Through our union with God*». We must see what that means and requires. Is that prayer? Oh yes. Pope John gives that example in the same document «Pacem in Terris»: «*Our prayer, he says, mounts to Him who by his passion and death, conquered sin, first source of all our discords, adversities and inequalities. We pray to Him of whom is said: «For He is our peace, who has made us both one, and has broken down the dividing wall of hostility... and He came and preached peace to you who were far off and peace to those who were near.*» (Eph. 2, 14-17). And Pope John believes in the meaning of prayer. And he is right. The same Spirit, who prays in us, is the God of heaven and earth. Praying we realize peace, we create peace. At the moment of our prayer we work out God's Peace! We shall come back to this element of prayer in our concern for peace. For the moment we will finish this subject of prayer with Pope John: «*We ask in our prayer that God may banish out from men that which may endanger peace, and that He may transform all men into witnesses of truth, justice and fraternal love. May God enlighten those who despair about man's destiny. May Christ inflame the hearts of all men and make them overthrow the barriers which create division, strengthen the bonds of mutual love, understand each other and forgive*».

II. The deeper causes of the imminent danger of war.

Before coming to spiritual remedies we have to point to the deeper causes of the imminent danger of war. Excellent efforts have already been made by Institutes, Groups, Congresses and Symposia to deal with Peace and Spirituality. And as it is not necessary to do double work, I'll use these sources frequently to introduce the work of this workshop. As these sources have to be known, I'll mention three of them briefly.

1) «World conference on religion and peace». World Conferences in Kyoto (1970), Louvain (1974), Princeton (1979).

2) International Colloquium, organized by Pro Mundi Vita in 1977 in Louvain on «The Christian Quest for Wholeness».

3) Interuniversitair Instituut voor Missiologie en Oecumenica. Leiden. Nederland. 'Exchange' Bulletin of third world Christian Literature. Nr. 18 (1977): «Spirituality and struggle for Fulness of Life» by F.J. Verstaelen.

The deeper causes which threaten peace have been summarized by the organisation of the International Colloquium on «The Christian Quest for Wholeness» as follows: «*Day and night we are faced with brokeness, loneliness, injustice - a vast kenotic awareness-; we are forced into a wild circus where people celebrate the destruction of life, beauty, wisdom and love. People, called to be free and free others, imprison themselves. We are strangers in our own world, and the tents we put up are burned down every morning. We build huge cities where children cannot play nor flowers get any sun; we poison wells and rivers with products meant to clean our clothes and we fill the air with dust and noise. We exploit and alienate, and we do this as persons, as groups, big organizations, multinationals, trade unions, as well as churches. With Harry Nouwen we recognize ourselves in the words of a modern song: «Confusion will be my epitaph/ As I crawl along a cracked and broken path./ If we can make it we can all sit back and laugh/ But I fear tomorrow I'll be crying,/ Yes, I fear tomorrow I'll be crying.*»

We find ourselves being caught in the prisons of huge, centuries-old collective consciences creating animosity and enmity between races, sexes, peoples, cultures, classes, religions and churches. We are strangers to our parents, our children, our husbands and wives. And every increase of knowledge and awareness deepens the experience of homelessness (P. Berger). Even though we forget our emptiness and hide our desires under a mountain of needs, satisfying them with greater and greater consumption of things and of persons, we reawaken in a deeper void and closer despair.

«The acceptance however of this open wound in our self, in the self of our friends and communities, in the heart of mankind, is a necessary starting point for an experience of true healing», said Prof. Kerkhofs in the opening-speech we quoted above.

The void of men calls for fulness; frustration calls for wholeness; the broken body of mankind calls for healing; personal salvation for social salvation; rationality for spirituality; the seen calls for the Unseen, the graspable for the Ungraspable.

III. Religious peace movements need deeper remedies for deeper causes of the danger of war. Spirituality.

Spirituality? What does it mean? Spirituality is in the first place a basic human category, an anthropological structure. The Indian theologian, Mr. M. Thomas, quoted by Verstaelen in 'Exchange' put it in these terms: *«Human spirituality is the way in which man, in the freedom of his self transcendence, seeks a structure of ultimate meaning and sacredness within which he can fulfil or realize himself in and through his involvment in the bodily, the material, and the social realities and relations of his life on earth».* From the Will to Power we are at long last beginning to see the possibility of a conversion, a turnabout to a Will of Meaning, says Frederick Franck in «The Whole Earth Papers»

Nr. 14 in an article written by him: 'The human image'. *«Isn't a priority...for everyone with any influence on our culture, to encourage and nurture this will to Meaning wherever it occurs, and regardless of the label it carries?».* *«Everywhere,* says Franck, *I see signs of this mutation which longs to find a way out of the trap of that nihilism, that Will to Power, that Will to Death, which has brought us to this Ultimate Impasse and replace it by a Will to Meaning, a will to Life».*

Thus 'spirituality' is defined, pragmatically and even phenomelogically, as being one typical way of handling the human condition. If you prefer to put it in more religious terms, you may say that it represents man's basic attitude vis-à-vis his Ultimate End (cf. Panikkar in 'The Trinity and World Religions).

I'll finish this paragraph with an important remark of the World Conference on Religion and Peace III, by saying that *«Spirituality is present in all people of good will; in theîsts as they imbue life with their experience of the divine presence, and in Atheîsts (even though many might not admit it) with concern for the destiny of humanity. These may be said to constitute the vertical and horizontal axes of the approach to the problems of humanity. These converge in an ultimate concern which is the common call to responsibility. Spirituality, then, may be defined as the consciousness of responsibility (including responsibility for restructuring political and economic institutions) rooted in one's experience of the divine. Spirituality is to be considered from two angles: an individual's direct communication with the divine and a group's combined effort to develop a relationship with the divine for the promotion of internal peace of mind. There may be, in certain traditions, no difference between the truly spiritual person and the divine. For this transformation the person has to be purified».*

The WCRP-report continues: «*Dividing the subject of spirituality into three manifestations - meditation, prayer, and silent reflection - is a Western way not sufficiently rich. A fuller understanding includes regular spiritual exercise and withdrawal of one's thoughts from a materialistic environment. Training for this should commence with children as they are closest to the divine. The aim should be to reconcile physical existence with spiritual reality of the divine. Wars are planned in the minds of the individuals. So peace can be planned by individuals and spread. Hence, spiritually-activated individuals remaining non-violent can physically spread the ideology far*».

«*Through meditation, prayer, silent reflection, and spiritual exercise, we open ourselves to the activity of the divine which effects radical transformation of the person, a surrendering of self to the divine will. Thus we believe that the revitalization of our spiritual life through meditation, prayer, silent reflection and spiritual exercises is a fundamental matter in our struggle for world-peace and justice. It is not an activity to hide from the world, but a discipline to prepare us for the world and empower our work in the world, and the vehicle that will inevitably propel us into the world*».

The WCRP-document concludes with a call for Interfaith Meditation: «*Collective interfaith meditation among persons of different traditions promotes the unity of the human family. For the promotion of peace among communities, all efforts must be made to expand collective meditation in different localities... Congregational prayer brings the groups close to the divine and also persons in a group close to each other. Interfaith congregational prayers will bring together persons of different traditions... and promotes togetherness*».

Recently I myself could experience the strong effect of Interfaith Meditation. I made twice a meditative retreat of nearly a week with Tibetan Buddhist monks, Hindu monks, other Buddhist monks and Benedictine monks. It all finished in the famous mantra: «Om, may all the world be happy».

IV. Spirituality and the revolutionary process of our times.

Many will feel more or less uneasy, when we speak of meditation, prayer, silent reflection in connection with their engagement in peace-work. What is exactly the contribution of prayer, meditation, and silent reflection to the revolutionary process of our times? Some are sceptical. With all our meditation and all our spiritual efforts, they say, we have in the recent past made little advance towards a functional human order. Thomas Berry, theologian and one of the great creative thinkers of our time, tells us why. (Riverdale Papers V. 'Contemplation and World Order'. And 'Traditional Religion and the modern world' in Jeevadhara no. 5 (1971): «*The disorder of our times is largely rooted in the schisms between the secular scientific society and the spiritual religious society*». But then Thomas Berry observes that there is «*cynicism of modern man towards his own work. Though claiming to strive after a higher human process, he causes often a new agony to the submerged masses, e.g. in the great slums of our cities. Beyond this is the deeper tragedy of inner spiritual destitution that affects man even in the midst of his economic, intellectual and social success. The spiritual traditions of mankind, once they are responsive to the modern world, will be able to demonstrate a new creativity and redeeming vitality to realize the higher re-birth that is needed. A condition to succeed is that our spirituality understands the language and preoccupations of modern science. The scientific world about us seeks a solution of its ills by a scientific understanding of how the world came into being, how it functions, and how it can be made more effective in supplying the basic needs of man. It is the quest of a comprehensive story of the cosmic-earth-human process. Until recent times this preoccupation of man had the tendency to establish man's identity over against the earth process. But now this phase is coming to a close. Man is discovering anew his place within the earth process. He begins to realize that he is not the lord of the universe. He depends on the dynamics of the earth to sustain him in his own being and in all his activities. Man must define himself primarily in relation to the earth. Man is the consciousness of the earth*».

It is within this context that Thomas Berry likes to situate the type of contemplation that can be effective in assisting toward world order. The first thing to note is that «*the primary journey is not the journey of the human community, it is the journey of planet earth itself. So our contemplation should be a functional awareness of the primacy of subjective communion with the totality of things and with each particular thing. In all things there is a subjectivity, and man has to commune with this self, this centre of things with a profound intimacy. It is a contemplation whereby man sinks deep into the subjectivity of his own being. So man will experience the totality of things and constitute a truly functional world order*».

«*Finally in this contemplation and communion man will be able to absorb the new energies that are available to man in psychic order from his contact with the cosmic-historical process. Almost limitless personal cosmic power belongs to each of us if only we will absorb it*». (Pro Mundi Vita. Bulletin 69.

I'm sure that the great masters of Asian spirituality and meditation are very important to us to teach us the ways of meditation and prayer. So, in our Pax Christi Movement we will do well to have a common concern with them for peace on earth.

V. Liberation.

The term 'Liberation' is a key-concept of contemporary understanding of the christian call and task in a world full of poverty, exploitation and alienation of millions of men, women and children. The term 'Liberation' is linked with terms like 're-volution', 'struggle', 'combat'. How can a Peace Movement, how can Pax Christi handle these concepts which have clearly a political connotation? How can Pax Christi act in desperate conflict situations? Real peace is not to be secured through compromise with justice and essential principles. It is often tempting to seek a false peace, to seek reconciliation at the expense of justice. How will Pax Christi accomplish its task to discover creative and non-violent ways of dealing with conflicts. What kind of spirituality will help us to find ways to peace? Will prayer help to find these ways?

I'll quote once more from the WCRP III-Findings. Archbishop Angelo Fernandes in his presidential address to WCRP III stated: «*What is ultimately at stake is the salvation of wholeness of man both as an individual and in society. However, for religion to exercise its integrating power, yet another of its functions has to come to play, viz., withdrawal from the fray, or 'withdrawal and return' as Arnold Toynbee would have it, in order to get to the root of things that are happening. This situation or contemplation or silent reflection, call it what you will... Unless we recognize the vital importance of this 'inner work' and structure our socio-economic edifice and our very way of life around this realization, our human and social problems will remain 'unsolved and seemingly even as our efforts to solve them become more frantic*».

«*In our working for peace, the way we engage in it is less important than the spirit of our engagement. To attain any objective, violence must be ruled out. Coercion, though sometimes necessary, is not desirable; persuasion is more suitable. Even when persuasion is used, sympathy must prevail. We must learn to do justice to our friends and foes, to maintain all people as brothers and sisters. Through the basic philosophy of love, other people's pain must become our own. The role of prayer is to nurture that attitude. We thus develop tolerance with understanding instead of tolerance with indifference. For the former we must develop knowledge about each other's traditions. Then cooperaton in common concerns becomes easy*». Michel Mildenburger, in his article 'Spirituality as Alternative' (in the Ecumenical Review, July 1977) writes: «*If the line of meditative mystical experience impulses towards selfdiscovery and human wholeness, then this second line (= spirituality for combat) to some extent in the opposite direction, opens up the prospect of historical liberation and the experience of eschatological salvation. The metaphor of 'departure' and its complementary 'return', once again seems appropriate here. This excludes from the start any attempt to play off a 'mystical' against an 'emancipatory' spirituality or to set up any antagonism between 'Eastern' and Christian' spirituality*».

VI. Prayer: meditation, contemplation, reflection.

I take the term 'Prayer' in the title of our workshop as a classification. Meditation, contemplation, reflection are its specific forms. But Prayer stands also for oral prayer. This prayer may sanctify our activities. It may open ourselves and others to the working of the Spirit. But let us not supernaturalise too rapidly the ways of prayer and meditation. Our prayer and even our oral prayer exercise some earthly influence. Meditation and prayer do not eliminate the natural, but fulfil it.

Once I stayed for a few weeks in the great spiritual center of Hinduism, Rishikesh, in the north of India. Whilst there I observed that every afternoon an important group of monks came together to sing mantras, repeating for a long time the same words of prayer. I questioned a monk what they were doing, and if they were praying to God? No, he said, one of our spiritual leaders lies seriously ill in the U.S.A. So we envelop him with our prayers for health. Another time I witnessed in the Tibetan Buddhist colony of Dharamsala that many monks gathered in the monastery where the Dalai Lama lived. The Dalai Lama was about to leave for his first journey to the West. I asked if all these monks from near and far had come to say good-bye to the Dalai Lama? No, they replied: we come to pray together and to create a strong favorable vibration around the Dalai Lama and around the plane in which he will travel, in order to be safe from all evil on his journey. Great!

It may be interesting to quote here the founder of Transcendental Meditation: «*The only golden gate to peace in life is the experience of transcendental bliss consciousness and this great glory of life is easy for everyone to achieve and live throughout life... the life of the individual as its every thought, word and action influences the entire field of the cosmos. Therefore, someone with peace at heart naturally vibrates peace and harmony to influence the whole universe... Is it not high time for all those interested in world peace to start from the individual units of universal life. Trying to solve the problems of international conflicts, while ignoring the level of individual problems is not an adequate attempt to establish world-peace*»

We cannot forget here that one of the main subjects to meditate upon in Buddhism is the meditation on peace. The very detailed methods to acquire and to diffuse 'Peace' are known. It is a 'breathing-in and breathing-out combined with thoughts of Peace:

> «*I am Peace
> surrounded by Peace
> secure in Peace.
> Peace protects me
> Peace supports me
> Peace is in me
> Peace is mine - All is well.
> Peace to all beings
> Peace among all beings
> Peace from all beings
> I'm steeped in Peace
> Absorbed in Peace
> In the streets, at our work,
> having peaceful thoughts,
> peaceful words, peaceful acts.*
> (La méditation Bouddhique. Paris 1974)

Maybe you want a more outspoken christian character of your meditation. I think your method of meditation does not have to change: but let there be at the center of your meditation a Peace whose origin is the risen Lord himself: «*Peace I leave with you... not as the world gives do I give to you*» (Jo. 14, 27).

My intention is to finish this note on Prayer and Meditation with an example which shows how christian contemplatives came to work for Peace and active Peace-workers came to meditation.

A coalition of 23 Benedictine Priories in USA, called the Federation of Scholastica, has come out forcefully on issues of peace and justice. One of the actions endorsed was a «Benedictine Peace Witness» at the Pentagon as part of the 1980 year-long organized presence at the Pentagon. It was organized by the Jonah House, a resistance community in Baltimore.

Conclusion of this paragraph on prayer and meditation.

I hope that it will be possible for our workshop on Prayer to stress that:

Meditation and Prayer do not damage the practical efforts for peace.

Meditation and Prayer, on the contrary, are an important basis for action.

Polarisation between those who accentuate meditation and those who accentuate the political approach of peace-work must be avoided at any price. With WCRP-Princeton we «*confess our failure as religionists... (that) too often religiosity has led to a religious power closed to the problems of the world; too often peace exists only on the ideological level; too often spiritual growth has not issued in social action; and personal peace has not connected with world salvation and world peace*». But we are also convinced that peace is only possible where strengthened by spirituality.

Meditation increases the qualities of peace work. It summons the will to meaning to balance the will to power.

Meditation can give a fine feeling for what may be done to promote peace.

Meditation and Prayer raised great peace-makers. To mention a few: U Thant, Dag Hammerskjöld, Gandhi.

Commenting on his work, U Thant once confessed: «*I wake up in the morning as a Buddhist and a Burmese and meditate for at least a short while in order to set my work, action and thoughts into the proper perspective. When I return home in the evening, I become again a Burmese and a Buddhist... But when I enter my office in Manhattan, you will understand that I must forget that I am a Buddhist and a Burmese. One of my duties is to receive many people... I must open myself to them, I must empty myself of myself...*» ('The example of a great ethical statesman: U Thant' by dr. Robert Muller).

Meditation is a remedy for what people call 'Doom-thinking'. Doom-thinking can be considered as one of the greatest evils of our time. «*There is no more future*». *No message. No paradise. No God. We are living the great démasqué. Where is God after Auschwitz? Where will he be in the nuclear destruction?* Our image of God lies in pieces. We circle all round a horrible emptiness. It is the threat to peace. And if we cannot find again God, the final destruction will come soon. We shall no more find God made to measure. We circle around emptiness. Will emptiness itself now function as an image of God? Our arguments will not find it there. But meditation can and will do it, building in this way a new and spiritual foundation for peace and peace-work.

VII. Recommendations.

In the footsteps of the Seminar B of WCRP III we may perhaps recommend to Pax Xi International:

1) to give more opportunity for prayer, meditation and spiritual exercise, during P. Xi assemblies. Particularly in great assemblies a special room could be provided for continual prayer and meditation throughout all the conference work.

2) to urge that P. Xi gives vigorous support to the annual Weeks of Prayer for World Peace. On those occasions P. Xi groups should invite the faithful of other religions to interfaith contact and meditation.

3) Pax Christi should encourage religious groups and communities to commit themselves to work for peace and nuclear disarmament, linking prayerful life and peace-making. Christian examples of such entirely committed communities are the above mentioned Federation of 23 Benedictine Monasteries in USA. The above mentioned Benedictine Sisters of Erie, Pennsylvania. The Osage Monastery of Benedictine Sisters of Sandsprings. OK. USA. The Brothers of Taizé in France. The success of such groups and centers (maybe very small groups of men and women) will be: a substantial opportunity for meditation and silence; concrete daily contacts with others in whom marked spiritual depth may be recognized; prayer, focussed on specific areas; leaders able to move from the depths of their spirituality to world vision.

Dear Friends of Pax Christi movement: being myself a monk, my last words are those of contemplative Thomas Merton, who died in 1968 in Bangkok on a mission for East-West Dialogue: «*What is the place of the christian in all this? Is he simply to fold his hands and resign himself for the worst, accepting it as the inescapable will of God and preparing himself to enter heaven with a sigh of relief? Should he open to the Apocalypse and run into the street to give everyone his idea of what is happening? Or, worse still, should he take a hard-headed and 'practical' attitude about it to join in the madness of the warmakers, calculating how, by a 'first strike', the glorious christian West can eliminate atheistic communism for all time and usher in the millenium?*

What are we to do? The duty of a christian in this crisis is to strive with all his power and intelligence, with his faith, his hope in Christ, and love for God and all men, to do the one task which God has imposed upon us in the world today. That task is to work for total abolition of war. There can be no question that unless war is abolished the world will remain constantly in a state of madness and desperation in which, because of the immense destructive power of modern weapons, the danger of catastrophe will be imminent and probably at every moment everywhere. Unless we set ourselves immediately to this task, both as individuals and in our political and religious groups, we tend by our very passivity and fatalism to cooperate with the destructive forces that are leading inexorably to war. Christians must become active in every possible way, mobilizing all their resources for the fight against war. First of all there is much to be studied, much to be learned. Peace is to be preached, non-violence is to be explained as a practical method, and not left to be mocked as an outlet of crackpots who want to make a show of themselves. Prayer and sacrifice must be used as the most effective spiritual weapons, they must be used with deliberate aim: not just with a vague aspiration for peace and security, but against violence and war. This implies that we are also willing to sacrifice and to restrain our own instinct for violence and aggressiveness, in our relations with other people. We may never succeed in this campaign, but whether we succeed or not, the duty is evident. Everything is secondary, for the survival of the human race itself depends on it». (Thomas Merton's Struggle with Peacemaking. By James Forest).

Dom Thomas Cullinan o.s.b.
EUCHARIST, ANAMNESIS, COMMUNION

When I studied theology X years ago it was still the custom to solve problems about the life of Jesus by using the algebra of his two natures. We drew on either his divine or his human nature as the occasion demanded. Why did he work miracles? Because he was divine. Why did he suffer in Gethsemane? Because he was human.

I remember quite early on, as a young student, feeling that there was something phoney in this. It was too easy. Somehow it missed the crucial point that Jesus was a person, and that it was this single person who acted, not his 'natures'. It was invigorating to discover that the real faith of the church must be able to say: he who is God died on the cross.

2. That theology of the two natures of Christ, which we inherited from centuries of western tradition, tended to give us an abstract theology, in which the *story* of Christ (as our own also) had no central importance. It was a theology of Christ abstracted from the actual circumstances of his life and story. It was a «job lot» theology which we carried through life, trying to apply it here and there. But somehow the theology remained intact whether we lived and applied it, or not.

It is this «job lot», academic, theology which is being questioned today by many who seek in the incarnation an interpretation of the experienced realities of life, not a ready-make kit to survive those realities un-interpreted. Our academic theology is being most criticised by theologians from Latin America and, now, other third world countries.

3. Perhaps the central area in which our inherited theology is up for question is our understanding of the cross and therefore of the Eucharist. Let me outline the question as it appears to me: When we recite the creed, the events in the story of Jesus, on which we pin our faith are all those events in which something happened to him - not in which he did something. Born of the virgin, (then a big jump), suffered under Pilate, was crucified, raised to life, ascended to his Father. Likewise in the first three Eucharist prayers, when we make 'anamnesis' (a calling to mind and making present) of Jesus, we call to mind the events which happened to him.

4. Now this is not an historical mistake. It is true of Jesus, and of each of us, that God really enters life through. It is only through the chinks in our armour, through our poverty, our abandonment, our acceptance of the unexpected and perhaps unwanted, our suffering, and above all our death, that God takes hold of and transforms our life into his own. If it was otherwise, if it was through what we set up, what we plan, what we live for, (however much these may be in God's service), then we would in fact (though *of course* not in theory!) be Pharisees or Pelagians. God would be an anxious parent watching to see whether he can commend us for doing his will. Not a living, active, God, but a teacher-cum-spectator.

5. If then God transforms and liberates our lives through what happens to us rather than what we do, why does it matter what we do? or whether we do anything? It matters because what we do, what we live for, what we decide and pursue creates the context which gives meaning to what happens to us, the chinks, the poverty, the deaths. A moment of silence can either be a meaningless void or a pregnant 'moment' (as in a piece of music). The context supplies the meaning. This is supremely true in the case of death, the ultimate 'happening'. Death receives its meaning from the life that precedes it. And the cross of Jesus received its meaning from that for which Jesus lived, from the time of proclaiming the Kingdom and the coming of the Lord's year of favour, through his challenge to alienated religion and culture, to the final non-violent stance for truth and love.

6. If we isolate the cross from the context of Jesus' pro-clamation and stand for justice, if we isolate his death from the context of his life, then we have the terrible spectre of death of God's son as a self-authenticating sacrifice. Somehow the Abba-Father of Jesus, the God who is Love, turns into the God to be appeased by the sacrificial death of his own son. The prophets and the psalms had warned against such an idea of self-authenti-cating sacrifice. Jesus likewise in his preaching; and he went fur-ther in implying that no prayer is self-autheticating, in other words that prayer is not an isolated aspect of life, but takes its authenticity from the continued orientation of life at large. Sa-crifice and prayer is the silence in the music. (It has to be ad-mitted, I think, that many theological treatments of the redemp-tion, of atonement, of satisfaction, have abstracted the cross from the historical context of Jesus' life.)

. 7. When in the Eucharist we keep alive the memory of Jesus - do this in memory of me - we are therefore keeping alive all the many facets of his life and proclamation. And for the pur-poses of our present subject, we keep alive the memory of Jesus as peacemaker, reconciler.

8. «*I come to bring not peace but the sword*». Reconcili-ation, for Jesus, had no bourgeois overtones of property-based security, no militarist overtones of balance of power, no fascist overtones of law-and-order at any price. Peace for Jesus pre-supposed justice, that is a love and recognition of people as people beyond the confining bounds of kinship, class, nationali-ty, sex. Especially it pre-supposed a recognition of and commit-ment to the oppressed, despised, outsiders. 'Peace' is in fact a very ambivalent term. It means many things to many people and depends, for its meaning, on one's basic understanding of who people are; one's understanding of 'man'. Jesus called to a 'populist' peace, demanding a metanoia on everyone's part, a love of enemies, a hunger for right relations, for justice, and an abandonment of vested interests. His 'peace' was the Jewish 'Shalom' rather than the Pax Romana of law and order.

If we allow our current mentality, of seeing people as economic units, to pervade our christian thinking, then our commitment to 'peace' will reduce 'shalom' to 'pax superpotentia'. Peace is not secured by the balancing tricks of the powerful and wealthy. It is a gift mediated through the lives of the poor.

The irony of Jesus' peace was that it questioned and threatened the securities of people in all walks of life. It could not but be divisive. To believe with one's whole being, with one's heart and with one's style of life and with one's decisions in life, that if God is God then people matter most, - to believe that, is to be drawn away from all the illusory securities, the false 'peace', which the world can offer and which seem so plausible. 'Peace' dependent on status, income, security, standard of living. To follow Christ is to have *that* sort of peace shown up as illusion. What a sick joke. In the world one no longer finds peace - but fear not. My peace I give you.

9. The peace of Christ, Pax Christi, pre-supposes engagement. It is never a ring road round the outskirts of the city. I believe a person cannot be non-violent until he or she can be violent. The special character of the peace and non-violence of Christ is that it lies within and beyond, but never beside, a truly incarnational and political involvement with and for people. It is born out of the fire in the belly, out of the agony of sensing God at the heart of things, out of the painful dialectic between the market place and the desert. We make 'anamnesis' because we have 'koinonia' with people. Keep alive the memory of Jesus for communion.

10. Perhaps in the end we cannot work for peace any more than a painter can paint a picture to be beautiful. The painter must seek other things, to be true to his materials, loving of his subject, etc, and beauty is the gift. The peace which Christ gives is the gift, always surprising, which emerges within us and among us, when we have given our lives to what is true, what is just, what is loving among people. *'My peace I give you'*.

Fr. Donal O'Mahony o.f.m.cap.
ST. FRANCIS, PEACE SPIRITUALITY
AND LIFE-STYLE

It is fitting that in a congress devoted to peace spirituality, one paper at least be given about an individual person who lived it.

History throws up many possible candidates, but even allowing for the partiality of the writer, few would disagree that Francis of Assisi ranks among the outstanding subjects to exemplify in a person peace and peace life-style. But there is an additional reason for choosing St. Francis. This year the whole Franciscan movement, and indeed much of the world, will be celebrating the eight centenary of the birth of the Saint.

One of the recurring crises in our modern age is the need to simplify life style. It is an individual contribution we see all round in a sick society, turned in on itself, and wreaking havoc upon the rights and the liberty of both individuals and whole populations. Both capitalist and collectivist societies only further frustrate human expectations because they each emphasise «having» and neglect «being». However, there is no short cut to simplifying life-style. Cliches like «make love, not war», «flower power» hold no substance. Too many casualties have occurred when people opt out, motivated by glorious universal dreams, when in practical terms they are simply on ego trips, ending in disillusionment.

For the believing Christian who is adjusting or changing his life style so as to be in accord with his aspirations for world peace, the first and most authentic source he must refer to is the Gospel. In studying the implications of the Gospel for living life, one can approach it as a scripture scholar might do - identifying the various literary forms, interpreting words with background knowledge of Hebrew, Greek and Greek-Aramaic. Or, one can approach it more simply. Namely, in a spirit of faith listening to the inner spirit of the Gospel, acknowledging to oneself that the Gospel does indeed bear a message of God to man, but even more than that the same Gospel can effect a change in one's life, can transform it, because behind each word lies God's spirit, and it is God's spirit which gives life.

We are taking up the story of one person whose life was transformed by the Gospel message in this second sense. It is one of the most beautiful stories in the chronicle of Christian experience. The story of St. Francis of Assisi. And, hopefully, it has a very relevant significance for the Christian of the twentieth century. We will examine the man and his times; the form of his conversion; the social significance of his peace life style for the time he lived in; and, finally, the significance he may have for people who wish to deepen or even adopt a new and more fruitful life style.

First of all, the credentials of Francis. So many people, from the most diverse religious and cultural traditions, have written or spoken of Francis as one of the 'greats' of world history. Renan calls Francis «*the only perfect Christian since Jesus*». Gandhi praised him as one of the «*greatest wise men of the world*». Lenin is alleged to have said on his deathbed that «*in order to do what he wanted to do for Russia, he would need only ten men like Francis of Assisi*». Paul Chapman, a Baptist ecumenist has said that St. Francis and his movement is the natural bridge between Protestantism and Catholicism. Kenneth Clarke (*Civilisation*) calls Francis «*a religious genius - the greatest that Europe has ever produced*». Pope John XXIII went to Assisi to pray that St. Francis' vision would become the vision of the Second Vatican Council. The litany of praise is endless.

Francis was born in Assisi in central Italy in 1182, and died there in 1226 at the age of 44. Few men did so much to change society, and to change the lives of individual men, as did Francis. But he never forced anyone. His way, following his conversion, was a non-violent one. The only violence Francis used, a violence he exercised to the end of his life, was the violence which is in accord with the true spirit of the Gospel: violence to oneself.

Biographers describe Francis as a small sized person. Slender, yet strongly built. An oval face with dark eyes and short brown beard. He walked lightly, almost with a spring in his step and he was continually given over to sudden bursts of joy. Everywhere he went, people became attracted to him. They listened to him. While still a young man, a desire for justice was evident, mixed, however, with a passion for self-glory. Give Francis a cause to fight for and the baser side of his nature would be forgotten. He saw glamour in fighting for what he believed in, and it seemed to him a glorious thing to vanquish one's enemies by force of arms. On one occasion, going out to fight, he boasted to his friends «*I shall come back a great prince*». All this was before his conversion.

A type of despondancy gradually came in on Francis. He saw the futility of ambition. The hard, cruel realities of the battle field tore at his illusions and revealed the ugly face of strife between men. War dehumanizes. Did not Christ, he wondered, when disarming Peter 'ungirt every soldier'? Glory, which he sought so eagerly, could not be bought at the expense of maiming others. There must be another way. What way, he did not know, but at least he was open to a new vision, if a new vision emerged.

Then happened an incident of supreme significance. Francis was riding a horse in the open country. It was a beautiful Italian day. A sense of freedom caught hold of him as his horse galloped along the dusty road. Then bright as the sun on the road before him, walked an 'untouchable' leper. The sense of joy and freedom suddenly drained from the face of Francis, as two emotions clashed violently within him. Disgust at the sight of the leper, yet pity for the sore-covered flesh of the outcast. It was the emotion of pity which won the day. He jumped off the horse and embraced the leper. Reflection on this spontaneous emotion of pity over a period of time led him to a new understanding of Jesus on the Cross. Calvary was a self-giving, a magnificent act of love for human beings. And so it was that the crucifix in the little church of San Damiano became a focal point for nurturing his new vision. Looking at the crucifix, Francis saw someone who was great in his defeat; who loved his enemies rather than attempting to kill or maim them; who was strangely beautiful in his disfigurement... and who offered real peace to those who imitated him.

This vision of Christ crucified, which followed from his encounter with the leper, was not just a new revelation for Francis, but an invitation as well; an offer, perhaps the chance of a life-time. And Francis grasped it eagerly. He would adopt a new life-style. He would cease to be a supporter of the militant Crusaders, but instead become a crusader for peace. He came to understand, in a spiritual manner, that peace must be linked intimately with:

a) the salvation which Christ achieved for us by the Cross
b) love of God of which peace is the principal fruit
c) conversion of heart by which a person opens himself to the influence of the Holy Spirit, the giver of peace.

Today, however, we should not look back to those 750 years just out of pleasurable curiosity to see how a man lived in those times. What we have to try and catch today is the spirit of Francis, which captivated the imagination of the 13th century with its childlike simplicity and its Christlike freedom. For to hearken back to the simple, rural, idyllic setting of the 13th century Italy, with its rolling Umbrian plains, is of no use in the 20th century, as we try to live and to cope with the forces of a technological society, an urbanised civilisation with an industrialised milieu, typical of our 20th century western world. It is easy to lapse into the «golden age» mentality and to imagine that all good things were there in the past, so it is backwards we must go!

But that's not the way of the human spirit, which is creative and moves forward relentlessly. No. If we look back it is because a person's ultimate value to the world is contained not just in the historic events of his life - which may be quite trivial - but rather in the ideals and values by which he lived.

The first, and possibly the most important, thing to be said of St. Francis is that he was not led on by philosophy or statesmanship or humanitarian concern. He was led by the Spirit. In his last Testament, he wrote «...*No man showed me what I ought to do; but the Most High Himself revealed to me that I should live after the manner of the Holy Gospel. And this I caused to be written down in few and simple words*».

The whole life of Francis was that of a living witness to the Gospel message. He didn't write much. His faith wasn't bookish. He just took Sacred Scripture as his guide in life. He was a thirteenth century translator of the Gospel. But his language was not Latin or Greek, Italian or French, but the language of *action*. He knew nothing about hermeneutics or programmes for demythologization. He read the Gospels simply and plainly. The Gospel is not a culture, it's not a philosophy, it's not a sociology, it's not a political system. It's message of salvation, an effective radical message to mankind. And his charism was to bear witness to the world that the Gospel can be lived, in any age and in any place. He *dared* to live the Gospel. He *dared* to let Christ take over his life, and was prepared to accept the consequences. It was this daring which made him such a significant peace person.

This is fundamental to any understanding of Francis and it has to be emphasised to give foundation for this talk. His was a life which was a supreme example of literal imitation of Christ and which, consequently, produced absolute originality. Everything else about Francis followed from this:

- his sense of brotherhood and sisterhood
- his freedom of spirit
- his incredible sense of joy
- his love of nature and affinity with animals
- his renunciation of power, privilege and possession
- his dedication and commitment to peace
- his desire to spread the Gospel to all nations
- his embracing of poverty as a bride - Lady Poverty.

Historical Perspective

It is important when evaluating Francis in relation to the time he lived in, to remind ourselves of some of the features of the 12th and 13th century society in Europe.

Firstly, it was a time when the ideal of chivalry and gallantry was still held in honour in Italy. The Knight in shining armour, the chivalrous soldier, was still the hero of youth. The knight gallantly protected the weak and conquered the aggressor by force of arms. In his youth Francis always aspired to be a knight.

Secondly, it was the time of the Crusades. These were so-called holy wars of that time. The Crusades had very far-reaching effects on European society, and gave powerful impetus to the collapse of the old, static order which prevailed. People came alive to the fact that the world did not end at the boundaries of their local lord's territory. There was a desire to travel, a spirit of adventure, the growth of commerce. New ideas were abroad, contacts with Eastern learning were renewed and through it contact with the pagan Greek wisdom of Plato and Aristotle. New luxuries, monies, silks and spices were brought in. It was a time of crisis because it precipitated the clash of two cultures - something not unlike our own time.

Thirdly, it was a time when there was a rigid class structure in medieval society. Society was hierarchical in structure - a kind of pyramid. Its unity came from one faith. The three main classes in that society were:

1) the *orantes* or men of prayer: bishops, priests, clerics, monks

2) the *bellatores* or *defensores*: the princes, knights and soldiers.

3) at the bottom of the social ladder were the *laboratores*; the workers, ordinary people, the farmers, the small merchants, the artisans.

The merchants, however, in Francis' time were on the upgrade. Businessmen, wool and cloth merchants especially were becoming more important. They were the *nouveau riche*, who *bought* status in a society which was in transition to an economy of money (as distinct from barter) as the ordinary means of exchange. Money was becoming power. It was also fast becoming a status symbol. These merchants formed a wealthy middle-class. They became more educated. They travelled a lot to foreign markets; came back with new ideas. Francis' father belonged to this class. He was the richest man in Assisi, and on one of his travels to France, met his wife to be. Hence the name «Francis» was given to their son. Francesco, literally meaning «little Frenchman».

But while Francis was born into this 'new rich' grouping in Italy, he was one of the rich ones who identified himself with the poor.

Some people say that Francis was a «poverty fanatic». But it wasn't poverty as such that he was interested in, but poverty in as much as he believed it to be fundamental to the Gospel message to follow the poor, humble crucified Christ. His dedication to Poverty is a direct result of his mystical identification with the poor Christ, naked on the Cross. The *poor* Christ, note, not the *poverty* of Christ. Poverty for Francis was not destitution. Poverty was something that was life-giving rather than life-denying. In a word, poverty was a practical sharing, which included detachment from possessions, in order that he could all the better experience absolute dependence on God's goodness, like Jesus did.

His vision of the world became all the more beautiful as he saw it through God's eyes. He could really say to the big property owners - in the words of the poet - «the land is yours but the landscape is mine». Part of Francis' revolutionary understanding of poverty was the refusal to be identified with any class and so he accepted all classes into the Franciscan Order without distinction ... even robbers! Other religious Orders at that time - the great Benedictine Order for example - accepted people according to their class - if one had a dowry or title one was guaranteed entry as a Choir Brother or Choir Sister. This may seem repulsive to our modern democratic sensibilities. But at that time it was all regarded as an expression of a properly ordered family. However, for Francis, all people were brothers and sisters, because they were the Sons and Daughters of God. They were equal in the sight of God and that is all that mattered. He frequently repeated to the friars: «What a man is in the sight of God, so much he is, and no more». So, Francis took a stand on the two things which enabled people to acquire power or dominion over other human beings:

a) the feudal system of *property ownership* which gave power and prestige to the minority

b) the *money* gained by the growth of commercial capitalism.

Francis had experienced the intoxication of commercial success in his own family. He saw its inherent dangers. For Francis, it's not what you *have* that counts but what you *are* - in particular what you are under the naked light of God.

In this Francis was prophetic. Intuitively he grasped the dangers of incipient capitalism. He had a presentiment of the fruits it would bear in time - as it most certainly did with the growth of industrialism in 18th century England, and later in other countries when social and economic relations became largely based on a narrow, pecuniary view of human labour - a «cash-nexus» outlook (Carlyle) - and on a negative individualistic,*laissez-faire* idea of economic liberty which lies at the root of so much violence and bloodshed.

Francis didn't despise money as such. He despised it only in as much as it was a means whereby one man could control the destiny of another. Francis didn't despise property as such. He despised it in as much as it was a symbol of political power, prestige and domination.

The poverty of Francis expressed itself in his renunciation of the false prestige of knight-errantry, of bourgeois values, of triumphalism, ambition, privileges and the force of arms. It was a renunciation of the condition of lord and master, and an option for the role of servant. More positively, it became his way of demonstrating that God, the Creator of the Universe, was a providential Father, and that everything superfluous belongs to the poor and needy, not only in charity but in justice.

The challenge of Francis to his times, then, though political as it had to be in its implications, was always a positive one based on his very personal identification with the poor Christ. He rarely criticized others, and in his writings there is not a single criticism of the Church or its Ministers, despite the fact that the Church was in such great need of reform. He simply responded to an urgent call from God to bring Christ to the Church and to mankind by presenting them with the freshness of the Gospel ideal. It *had* the appearance of freshness, a new Spring in the Church.

All of this had some very practical consequences, both for Francis and the people who followed him, as well as for peace.

Look at Francis after he had acquired this special relationship with God through imitating the poor Christ. All life was transformed and became, as it were, sacramental. No longer could he fight nor even hurt another creature maliciously. Every creature he saw had a quasi-sovereign claim to its own life, and anything contrary to this sentiment was sort of sacrilege. He would place a worm off the road for fear it would be trampled to death. On seeing a tree being cut down, he would beg of the wood-cutter that at least one shoot be left to carry on the cycle of life. But when it came to the individual person, nothing was good enough. To him a person was always unique, unrepeatable and never disappeared in a dense crowd any more than in a desert. Chesterton, in his Life of Francis, put it this way:

« What gave Francis his extraordinary personal power was this: that from the Pope to the beggar, from the Sultan in his pavilion to the ragged robbers crawling out of the wood, there was never a man who looked into these brown, burning eyes without being certain that Francis was really interested in him; *in his own inner individual life ... that he himself was being valued and taken seriously and not merely added to the spoils of some special policy or the names in some clerical document».*

Social significance of Franciscan Peace

Imitating the poor, humble Christ as a means to deeper communion with God and offering fresh possibilities of loving, had an extraordinary social significance for peace during the lifetime of Francis. Apart from helping him in his role as a mediator in conflict situations between neighbouring cities, it indirectly hastened the breakdown of a feudal system in Italy, with all its inherent violence and injustice. Francis sadly saw how many ordinary people died or were maimed by these wars which perpetually went on between the feudal lords, and for which people were conscripted. And, so in a Rule which he composed for the Third Order (the Franciscan lay movement) in 1221, Francis inserted this simple but dynamic prescription: *« You are not to take up lethal weapons, or bear them about against anybody».*

Such a prescription was a radical departure for that time of history. It enraged the feudal Lords, so much so that the Lords tried to force the individual members of the Franciscan lay movement to take up arms and fight, as they always did, their petty wars. However, the followers of Francis appealed to the Bishop of Rimini. The Bishop referred the matter to the Pope, Honorius III, who, on December 16th, 1221, declared that all followers of Francis were to be exempted from the oath of fealty, and thus from military service. The non-military status of all Franciscans was assured. So one could say that the conscientious objectors of the Third Order of St. Francis went some way towards smashing the feudal pledge by their refusing to go to war for their feudal leader. As a result, the power of the feudal Lord was taken from him. A victory for non-violence not often recorded by those who are sceptical of the values of such alternatives. Indeed, Gene Sharp's scientific theory that maybe institutionalised political violence is the radical origin of all war is somehow supported by this prescription and the consequences of this prescription, of Francis.

Francis placed enormous trust in the basic goodness of people. This followed naturally from his trust in God and became a fundamental mark of Franciscan peace making. What remarkable responses this evoked, even sometimes from the most violent. One classical example is to be found in his confrontation with the Sultan of Egypt. It was the heigth of the summer of 1219 and Francis found himself on the shores of Egypt where the 5th Crusade at that moment was maintaining a siege on the tripled walled city of Damietta.

Francis went to the leaders of the Crusades and begged them not to continue with their plan to take the city. Many lives, he said, would only be lost. The friar was not heeded and what he had foretold took place. Following a bloody battle, the Crusaders were driven back and about 6,000 of them were killed or wounded, not to mention casualties on the other side.

Francis immediately set his own plan into action, as the battle-line of the Crusaders regrouped to continue the siege against the Moslems. These Moslems, let it be remembered, were, in the eyes of the Christians, barbaric; a cruel, evil people who forced their captives to spit on the Cross and whose vices were a by-word. Francis, against all odds and every possible objection from Papal legate down to Army men, got permission to go through the enemy line. So Francis, along with another friar brother, Illuminato, walked barefooted on the hot sands towards the Moslem lines. The extraordinary sight of the two ragged men, unarmed and smiling, at least prevented the Moslem soldiers from cutting them down there and then. They thought «here must be a couple of lunatics», wanting to abjure Christianity and accept the Koran. So guarding them, they took the Christians to the Sultan's tent. The Sultan was Malek-el-Kamel, a nephew of Saladin the Great, the hero of the East. Given the nature of the religious and ideological differences between Christians and Moslems, the chances of these nondescript Christian friars reaching the Sultan's head-quarters were infinitely smaller than, say, that of an ordinary working man or woman of today making for China in order to lay before the heads of State some plan of how to achieve international peace.

What transpired in the conversation between Francis and Malek-el-Kamel? There is a lot of legend, but the fact is that Francis and Illuminato were invited to stay and subsequently were given a safe conduct to travel freely in all Moslem lands. The whole episode was commemorated on the Moslem side by an inscription on a tomb of a Moslem mystic, who was a counsellor to the said Malek-el-Kamel, which reads: «*His adventure with Malek-el-Kamel, and all that happened in regard to a monk are very well known*».

Francis, it seems certain, was the monk referred to on that inscription.

Are people engaged in violence today all that different? We too easily build up fearful images about them. This, in turn, breeds emotive responses which may be quite irrational. A cold war begins (no talking with men of violence under any circumstances), then comes savage labelling and, finally, a blind hate that is both unchristian and self-destroying.

There is a tale told of Francis about the fierce wolf of Gubbio who terrified all the townspeople. Francis went out to meet the wolf alone, talked to him and then made a pact that in return for regular meals he would leave the citizens of Gubbio alone. A Franciscan writer commented on this incident:

«*Francis felt sympathy for the wolf. There was something of the wolf in all of nature, that ravenous hunger, that restless pursuit, that baring of the fangs, so symbolic of what is wild and violent in all of us. But he saw in the wolf not so much the stalker as the stalked... He saw in the eyes of the wolf a fear, a hounted look, an anger and hostility that wanted to devour everything in sight in order to avenge his own hurt and alienation. Wolves, after all, are like men. If you fear them and ostracize and exclude them, they eventually turned into what you were afraid they were anyway*».

An incident involving Jean Goss and his wife, Hildegard, from Vienna, the former General Secretaries of I.F.O.R., is of interest here concerning non-violent Franciscan revolution (if we can call it that). Jean Goss and his wife met the so-called terrorist Camilo Torres in South America. Torres at the time had already opted for armed resistance when he received an unexpected visit from the two I.F.O.R. people. They both explained their conception of non-violent Franciscan revolution and it appears that Camillo Torres in South America. Torres at the time had already days later, when they announced that they had to move on, he urged them to remain for a while longer. His actual words were: «*Stay with us for a month longer and talk to us about Franciscan non-violent revolution*», adding «*I think I might be converted to your viewpoint once I come to appreciate how it works*». Unhappily, they were unable to do so.

Today the whole area of violence is the subject of much research work by professionals. But St. Francis and his way of peacemaking has, one feels, something special to offer. His non-violent life style helped to change not only lives of individuals but initiate revolutionary changes in society. This life style did not depend on words or preaching, but on doing. No one better than St. Francis could the saying be applied to: «*What you are thunders so loud I can't hear what you say*».

Francis saw clearly, when looking at the crucifix in San Damiano, why Christ choose to be poor. Holy Scripture states it in this way: «*Though He was rich, for our sake He became poor, so that by His poverty we might become rich*». In a word, if Jesus took on the condition of total dependence and absolute emptiness before God, His Father, then this should characterise his own person also, and indeed all humanity. That, Francis saw was the only way for a person to acquire a right relationship with people which is so necessary for peace. And the key to a peace life style also?

It also helps to create a right relationship with nature. Hence Francis could write one of the great medieval poems, the Canticle of the Sun, which to this day is fresh and beautiful to read and in which he refers lovingly to Brother Sun and Sister Moon.

Concluding remarks

One of the obvious limitations of this paper, based on the peace spirituality of St. Francis, is that it does not take into account the new insights gleaned from today's liberation theology. Francis, or indeed any of the saints in the history of the Church, did not attempt to achieve a synthesis between the mystical and the political as they are understood today. But that by no means invalidated the Franciscan approach. Indeed, in our opinion, it gives a very sound foundation for liberation theology and political holiness. So, rather than spelling out practical guidelines about how to live a peace life style in the 20th century, we will conclude this talk by giving a summary of the principles underlying the pilgrim life style of St. Francis. Each of us must adjust to

our individual circumstances in such a way that - without slavish-
ly trying to imitate the life style of Francis - we may nonetheless
learn from the spiritual and practical way which Francis met the
problems of his age.

1) Francis knew well that only one who is himself free of
the debilitating influence of riches and egoism can understand
the needs of those who have less. Poverty, for Francis, was not
primarily «not having» but rather sharing and living in such a
way as to call nothing his own. Like Jesus, he would then be
better able to depend on God's bountiful goodness.

2) Francis had a vision of human beings which was pre-
dominantly optimistic. He loved people. Christian brotherhood
and sisterhood had an absolute value. The notorious problem of
the conflict between spirit and body (which derived from Greek
dualism) is transcended to a degree unexcelled in the entire
ascetic and mystical literature of Christendom. The human body,
for him, must be evaluated on the basis of its similarity to
Christ's Body, rather than on its relation to the material world.
Consequently, he had an unconditional respect for every person
from Pope to robbers, the poor and wealthy, the believer and un-
believer. The priest and the leper, however, were particularly
special. The priest because he made present the Body and Blood
of Christ in the Eucharist; the leper because he symbolised the
outcast.

3) Francis had a close personal identity with Mother
Earth. Everything on this earth was beautiful, pure, precious and
revelatory of our Lord. He was a champion environmentalist.
The whole physical world was to him a sort of gigantic natural
monstrance of the Incarnate Word. All creatures were his
'brothers' and 'sisters' because they shared with him:
  a) a common origin
  b) the gift of existence and destiny
  c) symbols and bearers of Christ, the first born brother of
every creature.

4) Francis had a unified world-view. For this reason he could never justify war as a means of peace. War was a collective sin, destruction of love. War is the opposite of peace which, in biblical language, is the fruit of love, the supreme evangelical law.

5) So convinced was Francis that the source of peace could only be found in God that he greeted every confrere and stranger alike with the words «*The Lord give you His peace*». In fact this greeting extended even to creatures. One cannot help smiling at the fact that when Francis returned from the East in 1220 he betook himself to Pope Honorius III and greeted him with the words «*Holy Father, may God give you peace*», while a short time before that - an authoritative source comments - Francis, the brother of all creatures 'in the usual way' addressed a great flock of birds gathered in a field, with the greeting «*The Lord give you peace*».

Today our modern person is often alienated not only from God but from himself and his environment. We are sorely in need not only of peace, love and reconciliation, but also new communities in which the spirit of Christianity and Francis may provide a living example of what it means to be human. Francis of Assisi was «brother» to every human - and to everything. He loved the earth. He loved the sky. He loved animals and insects and people and cities. He was, wrote Michael Novak, «*one of the two or three Christians in whom Christianity most nearly reached its fullness. He is our western Gandhi, our own Sidartha, our most loving imitator of the Lord*».